THE NEW MONEY MANAGEMENT

WILEY FINANCE EDITIONS

WILEY FINANCE EDITIONS

THE NEW MONEY MANAGEMENT
A Framework for Asset Allocation

Ralph Vince

JOHN WILEY & SONS, INC.
New York • Chichester • Brisbane • Toronto • Singapore

Copyright © 1995 by Ralph Vince
Published by John Wiley & Sons, Inc.

Library of Congress Cataloging-in-Publication Data:

Vince, Ralph, 1958–
    The new money management : a framework for asset allocation /
Ralph Vince.
      p. cm.—(Wiley finance editions)
    Includes bibliographical references.
    ISBN 0-471-04307-9
    1. Money management. 2. Asset allocation. I. Title.
II. Series.
HG4529.5.V56   1995
332.6—dc20   94-31463

Up ahead they's a thousan' lives
we might live,
but when it comes,
it'll on'y be one.
—*John Steinbeck,* The Grapes of Wrath

Acknowledgments

There are a few individuals who have helped me with or influenced my thinking in putting this book together. Unfortunately, many of them are working for financial institutions, and, therefore, their names cannot be mentioned. Nonetheless, they know who they are, they have my many thanks, and their influences are woven throughout this book. This is the product of far more than just my own individual input, and, unfortunately, this is a world where giving these people the credit they deserve would be to simultaneously cause them harm. That is the last thing I would care to do.

I must also thank those rare individuals at John Wiley & Sons, in particular Karl Weber and Myles Thompson, who, despite my Franco-Italian nature which makes me anything but easy to work with, managed once again to get this published. In late 1989, the original kernel of the whole idea was rejected in manuscript form by every other publisher but Wiley, who published it the next year under the title *Portfolio Management Formulas*. I have always found it interesting that the one whom I regarded as my publisher of first choice was also the only one willing to take a risk with the material in that first little volume, while those publishers of a caliber secondary to Wiley shied away from it. I am most fortunate that John Wiley & Sons has employed people with such patience and vision, and I am even more fortunate that they had the (somewhat) misfortune of being assigned to work with me.

I must thank my friends Dixie Jerdon, as well as Gordon Nichols, who have put up with me, and in some way, directly or not, influenced what has gone into this book. If I hadn't met Gordon back in my clerking days, I am certain I never would have followed this path.

Credit for the material in this book also goes to the guys at First October Trading Company, Fred Hawley, Dave Stasko, Greg King, Hank Gillette, and Chris Fleenor. They have changed the way I view the markets and life. I also must mention my Thursday afternoon lunch buddies, George Sommer, Dave Lange, and Harry Roegner.

I dare not forget to thank Ralph Vince I, "Bubba," my granddad, who in 1906, as six-year-old Raphael DaVinci, came to America and would later play in the National Football League against the likes of Jim Thorpe. I respect him more than I'll ever be able to convey to him. Though we disagree regularly, in my worst moments he has always been there to help me out.

Larry Vince, my father, would have loved this book. He deserves as much credit for it as anyone, having piqued my interest in optimal mathematical solutions at a young age with an explanation of the traffic flow and light timing on Cleveland's Carnegie Avenue.

I also must thank my mother, Rejeanne, perhaps the smartest person I know. I am not a very practical person in many respects. I say she is perhaps the smartest because she is by far the most practical. When I really have needed someone's opinion, she has always had the best, in terms of the most practical, advice. I only wish I could do the same for her.

Credit here is long overdue to Larry Williams for this book as well as its predecessors. Everything I have done in this vein has been spawned by him and his unique "child mind" curiosity. It was Larry who got me started on all of this, and none of it would have happened had it not been for my good fortune of having worked for him. This is every bit as much his product as it is mine.

I am also most indebted to Richard Wilkie, not only for the wonderful opportunity he presented to First October Trading Company, but also for his unwavering support through the drawdowns. I am most grateful.

These last twelve or so months have been particularly difficult for me from a personal point of view. I must thank, last, but certainly not least, Vickie DeWitt, not only for her patience with me while I was writing this, but also her help with this and everything else in what has truly been a difficult time. Her influence in this book, on me, my life and thought process, and I hope, her remarkable nature, permeate this book throughout.

I cannot thank you all enough.

Contents

PREFACE

This book is the third in a series of books on the *optimal f* notion. Actually, I like to think of it as volume three of the same book. As time goes by, the picture comes more and more into focus, and I can't help but feel that this is the definitive book on what started out as the optimal *f* notion. Some people may protest, "But you've written two books on this subject already; why beat the horse to death?" However, I simply haven't found anything more important.

This book ties together everything I've ever done. Everything I have previously written about on this topic simply laid a basic theoretical foundation for this, what I call a new framework in asset allocation. I think it is of such importance that it not only applies to traders of futures and options, but also to any asset as well.

Shortly after the publication of *Portfolio Management Formulas* in 1990, there was a good deal of criticism to the effect that trading at the optimal *f* levels will cause drawdowns in excess of most people's tolerance, and, therefore, the entire notion was flawed.

This made me angry, not only at these people's ignorance, but at least equally so at my own ineptitude in presenting the material. "I know about the drawdowns!," I would protest, "This isn't a trading system—this isn't one way of managing your money when you trade!" I would argue. It seemed that people familiar with the book thought I was trying to advocate one way—a system, if you will—in which a trader could manage his stake to meet what I called *optimal,* but which was far too aggressive for 99.99% of the world.

It has taken me about five years, and a lot more work on the subject to rectify this. What I was really trying to point out in *Portfolio Management Formulas* was that we were somewhere on the *f* curve whether we acknowledged it or not, and, given the benefits and consequences associated with that, we can make a determination about what we are doing when we enter a trade. In other words, I was trying to show what I now know to accurately call a *framework.*

A *framework* is a way of looking at things—it is a perspective, yet it is more than that. It is a way to measure and to understand, often visually, the consequences and results of our actions in such a way that we acquire information about our actions which we otherwise would not obtain unless we were observing them within the given framework.

A *framework* is a way of looking at the benefits and consequences of our actions that applies to all of us when we trade, whether we acknowledge it or not. The *model* is a new way of constructing an asset allocation model so we can view things within this new framework.

This book is concerned with a *new framework* for portfolio construction, yet it also provides the model for doing this. The old framework, which, in various forms, has been in existence for the past forty years or so, shows risk and reward as competing entities. This new framework *does not* begin from that perspective. Rather, it concerns itself with finding the peak in an $n + 1$ dimensional landscape of leverage space, where n is the number of components in a portfolio. (The components need not be *market systems;* i.e., they can be collections of *scenarios* of outcomes for each component. This is important as it makes the book equally applicable to nonsystem traders.) The portfolio corresponding to this peak is the portfolio which is geometric (growth) optimal. This book will demonstrate a method (a model) for optimal portfolio determination under this new framework, which I call the leverage space model.

Secondly, anything I have written in the past pertained to asymptotic dominance. That is, the techniques I have written about in the past have all been ones that would yield the greatest return in the very long-run sense. This book is important because it will show how to achieve *continuous* dominance. That is to say, this book will show how to manage money in an account so that the result will tend to be dominant at any given point in time, not just the very long run. This is a giant leap forward for those who practice the methods in the real world; now a money manager can use a technique to ensure that an account will have a greater probability of being at its greatest equity at any given point in time!

I think this is a needed book. The older paradigms of portfolio construction regarded leverage only as a latter consequence in portfolio construction. This one addresses it in a foremost manner, and in a world where derivative/leveraged trading vehicles are becoming evermore prevalent, we can no longer relegate the leverage concerns to the back seat.

Further, the new model presented in this book carries some very interesting implications for the analysis exercise. That is, the new model implies that the analysis exercise isn't so much one of selection and timing as it has previously been regarded. Rather, the analysis exercise should be one of discerning probabilities of future possibilities. Under the new model, the analysis exercise can reap benefits beyond that of the earlier, simplistic exercises of selection and timing. The new model, fueled with the probabilities drawn from the analysis exercise, provides the selection and timing with a new mathematical rigor.

THE NEW MONEY MANAGEMENT

Introduction

GET OUT AND STAY OUT

Ultimately, all books are autobiographies. I'm afraid this one is no different. Around the time I was in eleventh grade, I received a letter from my high school, saying, in effect, "get out and stay out." It was a real head-cracking kind of place, an all-boys school run by Jesuit priests who had had enough of a wise guy like me.

That was about it for me and formal education. Not that I have anything against formal education. I may have been better off to have had a lot more of it, but those Jesuit priests were at odds with me and my tangents.

I was really lucky they did that. Any math I've learned I have learned on my own. I find that there is a fundamental difference between knowledge gained through formal education versus knowledge grubbed out of a dire need. With the former, failure presents the embarrassment of a poor grade. With the latter, it is an end to the world as you know it. That knowledge sticks.

Shortly thereafter I got a job as a margin clerk in the back office of a brokerage firm. It was a job which I at first despised. My job was to oversee accounts that were "okay'ed to trade" short options. Thus, my job was to oversee accounts that were doing any type of option strategy aside from outright purchases. The margin requirements were not yet computerized, so we had to figure the pairings of all the legs of option transactions in the accounts to come up with the lowest margin requirement.

The job got me thinking. As time passed, I found myself drawn to both the atmosphere of the place as well as the mathematics involved. Eventually, I got to like the job; I got to like the day-to-day action of the market. I liked the notion that the market was the fairest playing field of all—it doesn't care who you are, what your educational background is, your race, sex, age—nothing! It embodied opportunity. It was a giant, lumbering monster from another world—one who you could not take an apple to; one who knew nothing of anyone. It would just as soon smash you to pieces as it would reward you for taking risks.

I found myself looking forward to going in to work each day.

The microcomputer was just about to come out. Financial futures were in their early stages; options on futures and many other derivative products were about to be born. I naturally developed an affinity for both computers and the markets—a fortunate case of two things coming together for me at just the right time.

By 1986, I had the very good fortune of getting a 4:00 A.M. call from a fellow named Larry Williams. I knew who he was. He was the grandfather of nearly all mechanical trading systems. This was the eighties and things were really humming. Larry Williams was one of the bigger players on the managed futures block. To me, he was certainly the most interesting of the lot. Larry left some barely audible message on my answering machine about some trading system ideas he would like to see programmed.

The programming for him soon became full-time.

One thing about Larry Williams: if he had one hundred programmers working for him full-time it wouldn't be enough. Next to the North Pole, Larry's shop is one of the world's most interesting places. Inside his head is a thirty-ring circus, where he has all kinds of projects, from the ordinary to the bizarre, from trading the markets to finding where Moses crossed the Red Sea—all going on simultaneously. People from all over the world, each working on these different projects of Larry's, would be calling all the time. Brokers, mercenaries, scientists, and wackadoos. It was chaotic enough to almost send me into a seizure. Just on the market research aspect alone, Larry would have more going on at any one time than perhaps the research departments of most brokerage firms.

I watched Larry make (and lose) what I considered a great deal of money in the markets. He is one of the few individuals who really can trade at the full optimal quantities and go through the concomitant drawdowns.

One of the things Larry had going on was that of researching money management ideas. It was here that I was really able to sink my teeth in. It allowed me to take what I was observing in the markets and in his trading, along with my mathematical curiosity and the systems research that he had going on, and pull it all together in a delightful salad that appealed to me like nothing else ever had.

I was so intrigued by the notion of money management and optimal allocations that I could no longer concentrate on programming trading systems. It was time for me to pursue this niche full-time with all of my energies. It was something *I* thought was important.

IGNORANCE IS THE PROBLEM

Someone I cared a good deal about passed away some time ago as a result of a terminal illness. In an immense universe where matter can neither be created nor destroyed, it is a perverse, remote thought that (to me) the most precious thing in the universe, life, could be. This is logically incommensurable. Nonetheless, it was still quite a loss for me.

I cannot help but think that the problem wasn't that this person had this terminal illness. The problem was that I didn't know how to cure it, or that I didn't know someone who knew how to cure it.

In fact, ignorance is usually the cause of most, if not all, of my problems. Problems really aren't caused by poor health, lack of capital, poverty, prejudice, our own physical limitations, or anything else.

Ignorance—or lack of knowledge—may be your problem too. At this moment, you are oblivious to the fact that, due to the earth's revolving around the sun, you are whipping through space at about thirty kilometers a second! You are ignorant as to whether the earth revolves around the sun, when viewed from above the earth's north pole, in a clockwise or counterclockwise fashion. You do not know if time itself is continuous or discrete—that is, does existence occur in imperceptibly small "packets" like the frames of a movie film, or does it flow continuously?

You wouldn't read this book upside down, even though it's just as logical to do so as to read it in what you call the right-side-up mode. You wouldn't even think of doing this just to get a different perspective on things, even though, once you get used to it, it is no more difficult to do.

Because somebody says something is so, does not mean that it is true. Because other people accept conventions, does not mean that we have to, or that we will be better off accepting them. You think that timing your entries and exits will make you a good trader, because that is the accepted notion and what you have been told. You think asset allocation is an exercise of simply maximizing return and minimizing risk because that is the accepted notion.

So don't just accept what is in this book as truth. Go out and beat your computer to a pulp, or work the math out on paper, to prove the concepts to yourself. To do otherwise is to simply perpetuate your own ignorance.

This is a book about overcoming ignorance in terms of decision making under unknown outcomes, and, more specifically, determining optimal portfolios for trading the markets. The part where everyone is so ignorant is, except for a very few individuals, no one seems to realize how immensely important this is to a trader. It is the difference between life and death to a trader.

Market timing, ultimately, has very little to do with it.

STRUCTURE AND FORMAT

I wanted to reach as large an audience as possible, not only with this book, but with the earlier ones as well. That's why I presented the material in the form of a book. Books are far less expensive to the receivers of information, far more accessible, and, usually, far more enjoyable than other means.

There are a couple of terms readers of the first two books in this series may be familiar with that are worth reiterating for those who aren't yet immersed in the material. The first is the notion of a *market system*. This simply refers to a given market traded with a given approach. For example, if I have two approaches to trading, approaches A and B, and I have two markets I am considering trading, markets J and K, then I have four market systems. I have Approach A to Market J, Approach A to Market K, Approach B to Market J, and Approach B to Market K.

Next is the notion of *units*. A unit is the smallest denominational quantity you are willing to consider in trading in a given market. The specification is up to you, the user. For instance, you may decide that a unit is one share of stock, or you may decide it is the round lot of one hundred shares. You may decide that a unit is one futures contract, or you may decide it is one mini futures contract. Generally, the smaller you can keep the denomination, the better you will be able to implement the new framework.

There is plenty of math in this book—more than I would care to have put in, especially when I am trying to reach the layman, but all of it is necessary to adequately present the material. To counter this, I have tried to make the text portion as light, friendly, and enjoyable as possible—as though you and I were having a conversation, something which, if not done in the context of a book, would not be taken seriously at all. I hope this does not detract from the serious nature of the material. I personally feel that life is too full of wakes and funerals to begin with, and that fun is something you must create; it does not fall from the sky.

There is not any math that you cannot learn. Most likely, you have gone further than I in formal education. Don't be intimidated by the math—if you want to learn it, as I did, you can, no matter how complicated it may appear.

In the past, I have been criticized by some for my selection of mathematical notations. I have always tried to shy away from what I consider ambiguous mathematical symbols. An example of this is the use of certain symbols to serve a double purpose as grouping operators. Commonly used are the radical sign (where it is implied that the symbols under the radical sign are parenthesized together) and the horizontal bar for division (where the symbols under the bar, the denominator, are considered parenthesized together). Okay, they win. In this text, I will allow such ambiguous symbols to be used, but I don't condone them. If it makes life a little easier for the reader, I'll do it here. Furthermore, I will refrain from using the caret ($\wedge$) to denote exponentiation, instead resorting to the traditional superscription of exponents. However, I insist upon using the asterisk ($*$) to denote multiplication, instead of the cornucopia of symbols traditionally used to denote multiplication, which only create confusion. My point here is to dispel confusion—otherwise why not do the entire text in Roman numerals!

I am assuming that you are at least basically familiar with some of the concepts from the two earlier books or with articles that have been written by others about these concepts. Also, I am assuming that you are fairly well conversant in college-level math. Considering that you may not be, I must tell you not to worry about the math involved—let the computers deal with it—and instead concentrate on understanding the concepts.

I have tried to provide numerous examples. I want this book to be clear, direct, and to the point. I want to avoid going off on tangents, despite my natural proclivity to do so.

Hopefully, this book will be a mere introduction to an entire avenue that others may find rewarding in terms of new research ideas for themselves.

1

A New Framework

I didn't want to write this. I stated in my last book, *The Mathematics of Money Management,* that it was going to be the last book I ever wrote.

Some funny things happened.

People would call or write me. People who just devoured *ideas.* They are everywhere and they came from all types of backgrounds—doctors, dropouts, engineers, convicts, judges, traders, traitors, rogues, rascals, and raconteurs. These people are experts, not only in their own fields, but in at least one other field. Generally, they are completely self-taught in this other field, oftentimes being self-taught in their primary field. They are people who truly believe that there isn't anything they cannot figure out or understand. They need to be contemplating ideas, they need to be learning new things the same way most people need oxygen. I find myself drawn to these folks. Through my correspondence with them, much new material has come about—put into this book—and everything I have previously worked on in this sphere comes together herein. Although none of this is very complicated, some of it has nearly driven me crazy. I have literally searched to the ends of the earth to find some of these solutions—or near solutions—to some seemingly simple problems. I would have resigned myself to never looking at any of this stuff a long time ago were it not for the constant prodding of these types of people. They have caught my interest.

Since the 1950s, when formal portfolio construction was put forth, people have sought to discern optimal portfolios as a function of two competing entities, risk and return. The object was to maximize return and minimize risk. This is the old paradigm. It's how we have been taught to think.

Quoting from Kuhn,[1] "Acquisition of a paradigm and of the more esoteric type of research it permits is a sign of maturity in the development of any given scientific field."

This is precisely what happened. Portfolio construction, after the second world war, acquired a mathematical rigor that had been missing prior thereto. Earlier, it was, as in so many other fields, the fact-gathering phase where each bit of data seemed equally relevant. However, with the paradigm presented as the so-called *Modern Portfolio Theory* (a.k.a. *E-V Theory* or *Mean-variance model*), the more esoteric type of research emerged.

Particularly troubling with this earlier paradigm was the fact that the unwanted entity, risk, was never adequately defined. Initially, it was argued that risk was the variance in returns. Later, as the arguments that the variance in returns may be infinite or undefined, and that the dispersion in returns wasn't really risk, calamitous loss was risk, the definitions of risk became ever more muddled.

Overcoming ignorance often requires a new and different way of looking at things. The new framework seeks to find optimal portfolios, but not within the context of risk and return as competing entities.

WHY THIS NEW FRAMEWORK IS BETTER

For nearly four decades, portfolio construction was envisioned in a two-dimensional plane, where return made up the vertical axis and risk, actually some surrogate measure of risk (who knows what risk really is), was the horizontal axis. The basic notion was to get as great a return for a given level of risk, or as low a level of risk for a given level of return, as was possible on this two-dimensional plane (see Figure 1.1). This old framework has long been regarded as being as beyond reproach as Ceasar's wife.

The new framework to be presented is an altogether new way of viewing portfolio construction, different than looking at portfolios in a two-dimensional, risk-competing-with-return sense. There are a number of reasons to opt for the new framework over the old.

Under the new framework, E and V (a.k.a. AHPR and V) can be thought of as inputs to determining the *altitude* in a landscape.

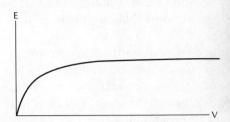

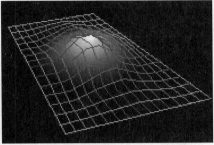

FIGURE 1.1 Conceptual view of the old framework, *left,* with the new, *right.*

The new approach is superior because the inputs are no longer along the lines of expected returns and (the rather nebulous) variance in expected returns, or some other ersatz measure of risk. The inputs to this new model are different *scenarios* of different outcomes that the investments may take (a more accurate approximation for the real distribution of returns). Now, rather than estimating things like expected returns and variance in those expected returns, the inputs are much closer to what the investment manager may be thinking, e.g., a 5% chance of an x% gain or loss, etc. Now, the investment manager can even account for the *far-out* slim probability scenarios as inputs to the new model.

What the investment manager uses as inputs to the new model are *spectrums* of scenarios for each market or market system (a given market traded with a given approach). The new model discerns optimal allocations to each scenario spectrum based on trading multiple, simultaneously traded scenario spectrums.

Furthermore, and perhaps far more importantly, the new model holds for any distribution of returns! The earlier portfolio models most often assumed a normal distribution in estimating the various outcomes the investments may have realized. Thus, the tails—the very positive or very negative outcomes—were much thinner than they would be in a nonnormal, real-world distribution. That is, the very good and very bad outcomes which investments can witness tended to be underaccounted for in the earlier models. With the new model, various scenarios comprise the tails of the distribution of outcomes, and you can assign them any probability you wish. Even the mysterious stable Paretian distribution of returns can be characterized by various scenarios, and an optimal portfolio discerned from such. Any distribution can be modeled as a scenario spectrum; scenario spectrums can assume any probability density shape desired, and they are easy to do. You needn't ask yourself "What is the probability of being x distance from the mode of this distribution?" but rather "What is the probability of these scenarios occurring?"

So the new framework can be applied to any distribution of returns, not simply the normal. Thus, the real-world *fat-tails* distribution can be utilized, as a scenario spectrum is another way of drawing a distribution.

Most importantly, the new framework, unlike its predecessors, is not one so much of composition but rather of progression. It is about leverage, and it is also about how you progress your quantity through time, as the equity in the account changes.

Interestingly, *these are different manifestations of the same thing.* **That is, leverage (how much you borrow), and how you progress your quantity through time are really the same thing.**

Typically, leverage is thought of as "How much do I borrow to own a certain asset?" For example, If I want to own 100 shares of XYZ Corporation, and it costs $50 a share, then it costs $5,000 for 100 shares. Thus, if I have less than $5,000 in my account, how many shares should I put on? This is the conventional notion of leverage.

But leverage also applies to borrowing your own money. Let's suppose I have $1 million in my account. I buy 100 shares of XYZ. Now, suppose XYZ goes up, and I have a profit on my 100 shares. I now want to own 200 shares, although the profit on my 100 shares is not yet $5,000 (i.e., XYZ has not yet gotten to $100). However, I buy another 100 shares anyhow. The schedule upon which I base my future buys (or sells) of XYZ (or any other stock while I own XYZ) is leverage—whether I borrow money to perform these transactions, or whether I use my own money. It is the schedule, the progressions, that constitutes leverage in this sense. If you understand this concept you are well down the line towards understanding the new framework in asset allocation.

So, we see that *leverage* is a term which refers to either the degree to which we borrow money to take a position in an asset, or the *schedule* upon which we take further positions in assets (whether we borrow to do this or not).

That said, since the focus of the new framework is on *leverage,* we can easily see that it applies to speculative vehicles in the sense that leverage refers to the level of borrowing to take a position in a (speculative) asset. However, the new framework, in focusing on leverage, applies to all assets, including the most conservative, in the sense that leverage also refers to the progression, the schedule upon which we take (or remove) further positions in an asset. Ultimately, leverage, in both senses is every bit as important as market timing. That is, the progression of asset accumulation and removal in even a very conservative bond fund is every bit as important as the bond market timing or the bond selection process.

Thus, the entire notion of *optimal f* not only applies to futures and option traders as well, but to any asset allocation scheme, and not just allocating among investment vehicles.

The trading world is vastly different today than just a few decades ago as a result of the recent proliferation of derivatives trading. Most frequently, a major characteristic with many derivatives is the leverage they bring to bear on an account. The old framework, the old two-dimensional E-V framework, was ill-equipped to handle problems of this sort. The modern environment *demands* a new asset allocation framework focused on the effects of leverage. The framework presented herein addresses exactly this.

This focus on leverage, more than any other explanation, is the main reason why the new framework is superior to its predecessors. Like the old framework, the new framework tells us optimal relative allocations among assets. But the new framework does far more. The new framework is dynamic—it tells us the immense consequences and payoffs of our schedule of taking (and removing) assets through time, giving us a *framework,* a map, of what consequences and rewards we can expect by following such and such a schedule. Certain points on the map may be more appealing than others to different individuals with different needs and desires. What may be optimal to one person may not be optimal to another. Yet this *map* allows us to see what we get and give up by progressing according to a certain schedule—something the earlier frameworks did not. This feature, this map of leverage-space (and remember, leverage has two meanings here), distinguishes the new framework from its predecessors in many ways, and it alone makes the new framework superior.

Lastly, the new framework is superior to the old in that the user of the new framework can more readily see the consequences of his or her actions. Under the old framework, "So what if I have a little more V for a given E?" Under the new framework, you can see exactly what altitude that puts you at on the landscape, i.e., exactly what multiple you make on your starting stake (versus the peak of the landscape) for operating at different levels of leverage (remember, leverage has two meanings throughout this book), or exactly what kind of a *minimum* drawdown to expect for operating at different levels of *leverage*. Under the new framework, you can more readily see how important the asset allocation function is to your bottom line and your pain threshold.

To summarize, the new framework is superior to the older, two-dimensional, risk-competing-with-return frameworks primarily because the focus is on the *dynamics* of leverage. Secondarily, it is superior because the input is more straightforward, using scenarios, and because it will work on any distribution of returns. Lastly, users of the new framework will more readily be able to see the rewards and consequences of their actions.

CONCEPTUAL OVERVIEW OF THE NEW FRAMEWORK

Suppose I offered to play a game with you whereby we tossed a coin and if it came up heads, you would pay me one dollar, and if tails, I would pay you two dollars.

You can determine the (arithmetic) mathematical expectation here, often called *the edge* (also referred to frequently in the literature, including this text, as simply the *expected value*) by taking the sum of the products of each outcome times its probability:

$$\text{(Arithmetic) Mathematical Expectation} = \sum_{i=1}^{n} p(a_i) * a_i \quad [1.01]$$

where n = number of possible outcomes
              a_i = ith outcome
       $p(a_i)$ = probability of the ith outcome

Thus, in our two-to-one coin toss, $n = 2$:

(Arithmetic) Mathematical Expectation = $.5 * 2 + .5 * -1 = 1 - .5 = .5$

Thus, you would expect to make 50 cents, on average, per bet (but only if you bet one dollar on each and every bet).

In this case, this coin tossing game, you would probably accept my offer. In fact, you would be quite suspicious of my offer knowing that if something sounds too good to be true, it probably is. That is exactly the case with this fifty-fifty game which pays you two-to-one, or any other game, including using a winning trading system.

Most people think this is a *good bet* because they have the edge. Yet, they are only halfway to the truth. Even if you have a game whereby you have an edge, you can still lose all of your money, regardless of how much of an edge you have or how big your starting stake, if you do not bet the *proper amount*.

Three guys go to a casino where this two-to-one coin toss game is being offered. Since this is fiction, we can offer a game with a positive (arithmetic) mathematical expectation. In reality, casinos could offer a game with a zero arithmetic mathematical expectation. Because each gambler has a finite amount of money, this creates a lower absorbing barrier which sooner or later would be hit—the casinos would still make money.

So our three fictitious gamblers, Larry, Curly, and Moe, go into a casino. Each is a different personality, with different attitudes regarding risk. Therefore, each decides in his own mind to risk a constant fraction of his stake on each and every bet. However, the fraction is different for each. Moe decides he will bet 10% (.10) of his stake on each and every bet, Larry settles upon 25% (.25), and Curly opts for 40% (.40).

The graph in Figure 1.2 shows this two-to-one coin toss game after forty plays. The chart depicts how much someone would have made, as a multiple of their starting stake, along the vertical axis, and what percentage of their stake they bet on each play along the horizontal axis. Notice that if you bet 25% of your stake on each and every toss, as Larry did, you would have made 10.55 times your starting stake. This was the optimal fraction (optimal *f*) to bet in this particular game. Notice that if you miss the optimal by only 15%, that is, if you bet either 10% or 40% on each play, as Moe and Curly did, you would have made only 4.66 times your starting stake. By being off only 15%, you wouldn't even make half of what you could have earned from this game. *Clearly, it does not pay to overbet.*

While at the casino they find Shemp, who has been betting 51% (.51) of his stake on each and every play. He has mistakenly thought that by simply being aggressive in a game where he has the edge, he will make his money grow faster.

Notice from the chart that at 50% or more you have an ending multiple less than one. That is, if you bet 50% or more of your stake, you will

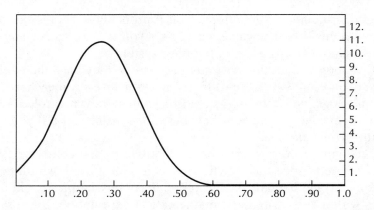

FIGURE 1.2   Two-to-one coin toss game, 40 plays. Ending multiple of starting stake betting different percentages of stake on each play.

go broke with a probability that approaches certainty as the length of this very favorable game continues!

Every game, every winning trading method, has a curve just like the one depicted in Figure 1.2. The points where they peak out, as well as the points where the line goes below one, vary from one system to the next. Yet, all systems have a curve with a single peak. It isn't enough to find a game where you have the edge. You must also wager the correct quantities. This very same principle is at work when we trade, whether we acknowledge it or not.

The fraction bet we simply call f. Every trader resides somewhere on this f spectrum, where:

$$f = \frac{(\text{number of contracts} * \text{biggest perceived loss per contract})}{\text{equity in the account}} \qquad [1.02]$$

This is so because the three input variables:

1. the number of contracts he is trading at the moment; and
2. the biggest perceived loss per contract; and
3. the equity in the account

are all givens. Thus, at any point in time, we can take any trader in any market system and assign an f value to him, to where he resides in the landscape (which is two-dimensional since there is only one game being played).

Whether a trader acknowledges this or not does not affect the fact that there is an f value associated with him and his position in a given market system at a given time. Even if a trader is trading a constant one contract, let's say, in soybeans, he is always at an f value. Suppose his system is profitable and his account equity grows, his f value will slide to the left (i.e., become lower) as his account equity grows, unless he steps up the number of contracts. Every trader, regardless of how he is operating, has an f value assigned to every position in every market at all times, whether he realizes it or not.

Why is this important? Because there is always a curve to this function, and it has just one peak (if the system is profitable). Where the trader's f is with respect to the peak dictates what kind of gain he is looking at, what kind of drawdown he is looking at, etc. For instance, if the trader is to the left of the peak, i.e., has a lower value for f than the optimal (in other words, has fewer contracts than is optimal), as Moe was doing, then he will reduce his drawdowns arithmetically while reducing his gains geometrically. However, if he misses the peak to the right, i.e., has a higher value for f than is optimal (in other words, has more contracts than is optimal), as Curly did, then he again reduces his gains geometrically, just as if he had on too few contracts; yet he increases his drawdowns arithmetically. Notice that Curly and Moe both had 4.66 times their starting stake after forty plays, yet Curly's minimum expected drawdown was four times as great as Moe's! It is obviously better to err to the left of the peak, having less quantity than is optimal, than to be to the right of the peak, having more quantity than is optimal.

At some point to the right of the peak of the curve, depending upon the system, the curve drops below a value of 1.0. This means that when trading at this level, as Shemp did, the trader will go broke in time with certainty. All systems, regardless of how good they might seem, have such a point.

All of this isn't to say that I have a religious belief that you have to be at the peak of the f curve. Rather, it says you can achieve what you want with this, but these are the tradeoffs involved.

By now you should see a framework beginning to emerge.

Notice then that where we are on the f curve is every bit as important as how good our system or approach to the market is, how good a trader we are, or how good our timing of the market is. A poor system, if only marginally profitable, can do very well if traded at the peak of the f curve. A magnificent system can do poorly if traded at the wrong f value.

In fact, it can lose money for the trader, eventually bankrupting him, if traded at an improper point on the f curve. One can only wonder why so much time and effort is spent by traders analyzing the markets and making trade selection when these exercises are no more important than quantity selection. Further, traders ultimately do not have control over whether the next trade is a win or a loss, but they have complete control over the quantity they put on that trade, which as an exercise of equal importance.

Logically, however, there isn't any reason to not be at the peak of the f curve. Notice that Moe is to the left of the peak. He obviously wants a straighter-line equity curve than the other players, and is willing to sacrifice gains on a geometric scale. If, like Moe, you want a straight-line equity curve, go out and buy 90-day T-bills; don't go trade a diluted speculative account (way on the left of the peak of the f curve).

MULTIPLE SIMULTANEOUS PLAYS

Now suppose you are going to play two of these very same games simultaneously. Each coin will be used in a separate game similar to the first game. Now what quantity should be bet? The answer depends upon the relationship of the two games. If the two games are not correlated to each other, then optimally you would bet 23% on each game (Figure 1.3). However, if there is perfect positive correlation, then you must bet 12.5% on each game. If you bet 25% or more on each game, you will now go broke, with a probability that approaches certainty as the length of the game increases.

When you begin trading more than one market system, you no longer reside on a line that has a peak; instead, you reside in an $n + 1$ (where $n =$ the number of market systems you are trading) dimensional terrain that has a single peak! In our single coin toss example, we had a peak on the line at 25%. Here we have one game ($n = 1$) and thus a two (i.e., $n + 1$) dimensional landscape (the line) with a single peak. When we play two of these games simultaneously, we now have a three (i.e., $n + 1$) dimensional landscape within leverage space with a single peak. If the correlation coefficient between the coins is zero, then the peak is at 23% for the first game, and 23% for the second as well. Notice that there is still only one peak, even though the dimensions of the landscape have increased!

When we are playing two games simultaneously, we are faced with a three-dimensional landscape, where we must find the highest point. If

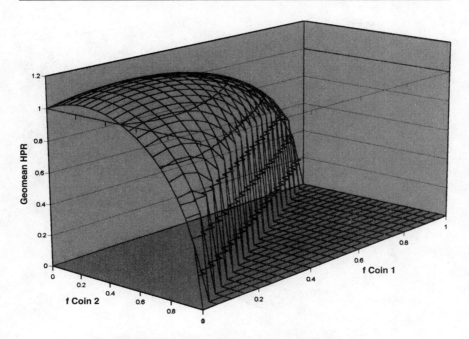

FIGURE 1.3   Two-to-one coin toss—one play.

we were playing three games simultaneously, we would be looking for the peak in a four-dimensional landscape. The dimensions of the topography within which we must find a peak are equal to the number of games (markets and systems) we are playing plus one.

Notice, that as the number of plays increases, the peak gets higher and higher, and the difference between the peak and any other point on the landscape gets greater and greater (see Figures 1.3, 1.4, and 1.5). Thus, as more plays elapse, the difference between being at the peak and any other point increases. This is true regardless of how many markets or systems we are trading, even if we are only trading one.

To miss the peak is to pay a steep price. Recall in the simple single coin toss game the consequences of missing the peak. These consequences are no less when multiple simultaneous plays are involved. In fact, when you miss the peak in the $n + 1$ dimensional landscape, you will go broke faster than you would in the single game!

Whether or not we acknowledge these concepts, it does not affect the fact that *they are at work on us.* Remember, we can assign an *f* value to

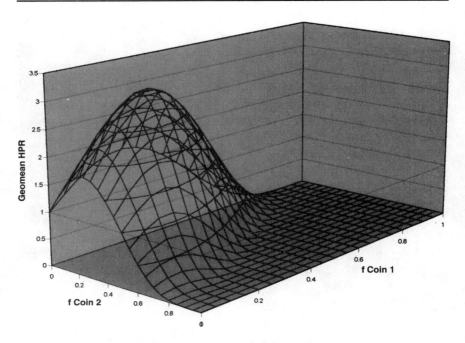

FIGURE 1.4   Two-to-one coin toss—ten plays.

any trader in any market with any method at any time. If we are trading a single market system and we miss the peak of the *f* curve for that market system, we might, if we are lucky, make a fraction of the profits we should have made, while we will very likely endure greater drawdowns than we should have. If we are unlucky, we will go broke with certainty *even with an extremely profitable system!*

When we trade a portfolio of markets and/or systems, we simply magnify the effect of missing the peak of the curve in *n* + 1 space.

A COMPARISON TO THE OLD FRAMEWORKS

Let's take a look at a simple comparison of the results generated by this new framework versus those of the old E-V framework.

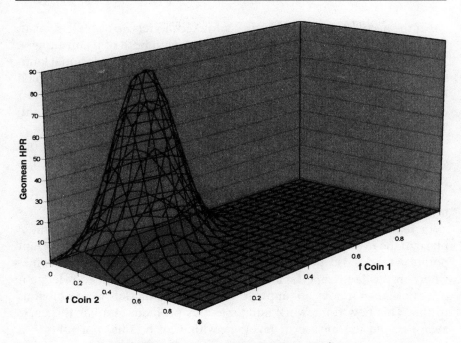

FIGURE 1.5   Two-to-one coin toss—40 plays.

Suppose, for the sake of simplicity, we are going to play two simultaneous games. Each game will be the now-familiar two-to-one coin toss. Further assume that all of the pairwise correlations are zero. The new framework tells us that the optimal point, the peak in the four-dimensional $(n + 1)$ landscape is at 23% for both games.

The old framework, in addition to the zero values for the pairwise correlations, has .5 as the E value, the mean, and 2.25 as the V value, the variance. The result of this, through the old framework, generates .5 for both games.

This means that one-half of your account should be allocated towards each game. But what does this mean in terms of leverage? How much is a game? If a game is one dollar, the most I can lose, then .5 is way beyond the optimal of .23. How do I progress my stake as I go on? The correct answer, the mathematically optimal answer with respect to leverage (including how I progress my stake as I go on), would be .5 of

.46 of the account. But the old mean variance models do not tell me that. They are not attuned to the use of leverage (with both of its meanings). The answers tell me nothing of where I am in the $n + 1$ dimensional landscape. Also, there are important points within the $n + 1$ dimensional landscape other than the peak. For instance, as we will see in the last chapter, the points of inflection in the landscape are also very important. The old E-V models tell us nothing about any of this.

In fact, the old models simply tell us that allocating one-half of our stake to each of these games will be *optimal* in that you will get the greatest return for a given level of variance, or the lowest variance for a given level of return. How much you want to lever it is a matter of your utility—your personal preference.

In reality, though, there is an optimal point of leverage, an optimal place in the $n + 1$ dimensional landscape. There are also other important points in this landscape. When you trade, you automatically reside somewhere in this landscape (again, just because you do not acknowledge it does not mean it does not apply to you). The old models were oblivious to this. This new framework addresses this problem and has the users aware of the use/misuse of leverage within an optimal portfolio in a foremost sense. In short, the new framework simply yields more and more useful information than its predecessors.

Again, if a trader is utilizing two market systems simultaneously, then where he resides on the three-dimensional landscape is everything. Where he resides on it is every bit as important as his market systems, his timing, or his trading ability. Where a trader is on the $n + 1$ dimensional landscape is at least 50% of what will make him a great trader.

The problem with all of this, which I readily acknowledge, is that regardless of the number of dimensions in the landscape, the peak moves around. That is, systems are nonstationary. Hey, I don't like this either. However, this does not negate the fact that there is still a peak to this $n + 1$ dimensional landscape that we reside in, and the payoffs and consequences for missing this peak are still intact.

Repeatedly, ignorant people—and I say ignorant because they apparently have not had enough real-world system trading experience nor enough virtual system experience via performing computer simulations of trading systems—make the false claim that "All systems eventually blow up." In most cases where people have made this claim, I have found that it is not that the system, on a long-term basis, has stopped making money. It may have temporarily stopped making money (i.e., a drawdown), but if the system is halfway decent, if there is a modest amount of *robustness* to the system, it will go back to making money—maybe not as much as it once did, but it will go back to churning out at least a marginal profit. No, it is not that the system has stopped making money on a long-term basis, it is that the peak of the *f* curve has shifted—to the left of where the peak once resided. Thus, a trader trading this system now finds himself—even though he isn't conscious of this—to the right of the peak of the curve, even if he were to the left of the peak of the curve to begin with!

So immediately we are presented with two problems: First, how do you find the peak of the curve in $n + 1$ space at any given moment in time, and, second, how do you predict where that peak is moving to? This book will attempt to answer the first question only.

TOWARDS A NEW TYPE OF ANALYSIS

In the old days, technical analysts were scoffed at by those who, by and large, did not understand technical analysis. Today, nearly every profitable trading entity employs technical analysis. Although there are still fundamental analysts, the spotlight has undoubtedly been taken over by the technicians.

No matter how good a system is, it will still make less money without finding the peak in the $n + 1$ dimensional landscape. Marginally profitable systems or traders can make infinitely more money than great traders or systems if they know the landscape better. The degree of profitability has little to do with the trader, systems, or concepts employed, but rather where they are on the $n + 1$ dimensional landscape.

Yet, people are still looking for better systems and methods of analysis. The situation is analogous to a person who is offered the two-to-one coin toss game and, while playing it, is still looking for a game that will offer better probabilities. He is ignorant of the fact that even if he finds a game with better probabilities, he must still find the peak of that curve. It also has a point where it will lose all of his money. Yet, thinking that the only thing he needs is a better bet, he is ignorant of the fact that the world is not flat. It is curved, and no matter what game he plays, no matter how favorable the probabilities, whether he knows it or not, he will pay a steep price for missing the peak of the curve of the game he plays. Worse yet, *the penalty he pays will grow as time goes by.*

Further, the measures used for system performance tell us absolutely nothing about the treacherous landscape we reside in. In fact, they may be more deceiving than anything else. A case in point is the system performance measurement of average trade. Yet, what we really ought to be looking at is the geometric average trade—how much you make per contract per trade, which is always less than the average trade.

Overcoming ignorance often requires a new and different way of looking at things, it requires that we adopt a *child's mind,* a blank page devoid of any assumptions.

Once the trading community tunes in to this new concept, once they realize that their world is not flat, technical analysts will go the way of fundamental analysts. Those who want to profit in the marketplace will move closer to the truth of what affects their bottom line, just as they did in moving from fundamental to technical analysis.

Once asset allocators tune in, they will see that portfolio construction is not an exercise in tradeoffs between risk and return, that optimal portfolios are not a location in the two-dimensional, E-V space. Instead, they will view it as a map of this *polymorphic* landscape in leverage space, where dispersion in returns (risk) is only a problem in that it reduces geometric mean return and alters the optimal use of leverage.* That is to say, dispersion in returns only lowers the relative altitudes in this landscape.† The trick is to find the peak in this landscape, not a comfort level regarding return and variance in returns, as asset allocation is conventionally practiced.

STATISTICAL INDEPENDENCE

Throughout this book we will assume that the sequence of holding period returns for a given trading approach are independent of holding

---

* Later in this chapter it will be shown that the geometric mean holding period return can be very closely approximated by using the Pythagorean theorem with the arithmetic mean and standard deviation in holding period returns. Thus, the arithmetic mean and standard deviation (dispersion) in holding period returns comprise the geometric mean holding period return, the altitude in $n + 1$ space.

† All of this is not meant to imply that risk and return are not inextricably linked—they are. If you want high returns, you must see high risk. However, I am saying that because of someone's ignorance of the topography of the $n + 1$ dimensional landscape in which they reside, they are probably not at the peak, and, thus, probably getting nowhere near the kind of return for the level of risk that they are really assuming.

period returns at any other time period, and are all independently distributed according to the same distribution.

There are many tests for statistical independence and tests of whether random variables come from the same distribution. We will not reiterate those here. Interested readers are referred to the two predecessors of this book, *Portfolio Management Formulas* and *The Mathematics of Money Management,* for more detailed discussions.

However, if there is statistical dependence of any sort, then the trading approach is suboptimal to begin with. The trader can then incorporate the dependency information into the trading approach to further enhance its profitability. Only when there is statistical independence can a trader, perhaps, state that he has no more work to do on his trading approach.

THE HISTORY OF *f*

Around the end of the second world war, a Hungarian mathematician named John von Neumann, along with Osker Morgenstern, introduced the world to the notion of *game theory* with their classic treatise on the subject, *Theory of Games and Economic Behavior.*[2] The theory was originally designed to deal with economic problems. However, this turned out to be one of the many great bonanzas of the twentieth century in that the theory has proved useful in military strategy, sociology, and politics, and it has given rise to such new fields as operations research. Truly, the limits of what game theory yields for us have not been anywhere near exhausted, much less explored.

Long distance communications were quite a problem around the second world war. The notion of transmitting data was fraught with problems in these early stages, not the least of which was the spurious, seemingly unavoidable electronic *noise* that interfered with communications.

In 1948, Claude Shannon published a paper in the *Bell System Technical Journal* entitled "A Mathematical Theory of Communication," which, in effect, kicked off what we now refer to as *information theory.*[3] In short, Shannon asserted that binary digits could be transmitted over a noisy channel with an arbitrarily small probability of error if the binary digits were suitably encoded.

By 1956, the two notions of information theory and game theory collided in the now famous paper of J. L. Kelly, Jr., "A New Interpretation of Information Rate."[4] Although the paper dealt with information theory, the upshot was that it showed that a gambler is better off to maximize the expected value of the logarithm of his capital. This was in direct contrast to what had been the accepted notion since the time of Pascal: that a gambler is better off to maximize the expected value of his capital, whereas Kelly claimed he should maximize the expected value of the logarithm of his capital. This then became known as the *Kelly criterion*.

Beginning with the 1962 classic, *Beat the Dealer,* by Edward O. Thorp, the Kelly criterion started to come out of technical obscurity.[5] It was Thorp who popularized the Kelly criterion. He really demonstrated the applicability and provided the workable formulas that the so-called *professional* gambling community devoured. The trading community, however, was very slow to accept all of this, and, despite Thorp's success in convincing the gambling community of the usefulness of the Kelly criterion, the trading community, following the high priests of risk control from the business schools, was essentially unmoved.

In 1980, Thorp published an article in *Gambling Times* detailing the *Kelly formulas*.[6] These were reiterated in Fred Gehm's now famous *Commodity Market Money Management*.[7] It was through Gehm's book that the trading community—that is, the speculative or commodity side—began to accept the Kelly criterion, at least in a small way, rather than the handful of mathematically oriented traders who previously accepted the criterion.

It wasn't until 1986 that a high-profile trader named Larry Williams began espousing the virtues of using the Kelly formulas. Shortly thereafter, it became difficult to find a seasoned speculative trader who wasn't aware of the Kelly formulas.

In short, the Kelly formulas satisfy the Kelly criterion, that is, they yield an answer we'll call f (as Thorp did), which is the percentage of your bankroll to invest on each play to maximize the expected value of the logarithm of your capital.

The first of these two formulas is as follows:

$$f = 2 * p - 1 \qquad\qquad [1.03a]$$

or

$$f = p - q \qquad\qquad [1.03b]$$

where p = probability of a winning bet

q = probability of a losing bet (since this is the complement of p, it equals $1 - p$)

This formula is only applicable, however, when you can win or lose the exact same amounts. For instance, if we have a 60% chance of winning one dollar, and a 40% chance of losing one dollar, we have:

$$f = .6 - .4 = .2$$

Therefore, we would bet .2, or 20%, of our stake on each play to satisfy the Kelly criterion.

When the amount won or the amount lost are not equal (or even when they are), the following formula can be used:

$$f = \frac{((b+1) * p - 1)}{b} \qquad [1.04a]$$

where p = probability of a winning bet

b = ratio of the amount won on a winning bet to the amount lost on a losing bet

Thus, for a game like our two-to-one coin toss mentioned earlier we have:

$$f = \frac{((2+1) * .5 - 1)}{2}$$

$$= \frac{(3 * .5 - 1)}{2}$$

$$= \frac{.5}{2}$$

$$= .25$$

Thus, we would optimally bet 25% of our stake on each play.

Note that the numerator in Equation [1.04a] equals the (arithmetic) mathematical expectation of [1.01a]. Therefore, we can say:

$$f = \frac{\text{the edge}}{b} \qquad [1.04b]$$

From this, the Kelly formula is also often expressed as:

$$f = \frac{p - q}{b} \qquad [1.04c]$$

Any of the [1.04] formulas will satisfy the Kelly criterion, or, as I say, yield the optimal f, regardless of whether the wins and losses are for the same amounts. For the [1.03] formula version, the amount won must equal the amount lost.

However, it has been my contention that these formulas are only applicable to a Bernoulli distribution, that is, a distribution with only two possible outcomes. Since most gambling situations have only two possible outcomes (a winning outcome and a losing outcome), there isn't a problem. However, in trading, there are many outcomes which a trade might have, and, therefore, I devised a formula which would yield the optimal fraction when there are more than two possible outcomes[8]:

To begin with, we must understand the notion of a *holding period return* (HPR). This is simply the rate of return on a given trade plus one. Therefore, a 10% return is equivalent to an HPR of 1.10, just as a 25% loss is equivalent to an HPR of .75.

But, the percent return we are using is a function of the value we are using for f. Thus, we can state that an HPR, mathematically, is as follows:

$$HPR = 1 + f * \left(\frac{- \text{trade}}{\text{biggest loss}} \right) \qquad [1.05]$$

Now, suppose we have T trades; then, we can multiply all of the trades, expressed as HPRs, and obtain the multiple we would have made on our starting stake, which we'll call the *terminal wealth relative* (TWR):

$$TWR = \prod_{i=1}^{T} HPR \qquad [1.06]$$

or

$$TWR = \prod_{i=1}^{T} 1 + f * \left(\frac{- \text{trade}_i}{\text{biggest loss}} \right)$$

Finally, if we take Equation [1.06] to the Tth root, we can find our average compound growth per play, also called the geometric mean HPR, which will become more important later on:

$$G = TWR^{1/T} \qquad [1.07]$$

or

$$G = \left(\prod_{i=1}^{T} \left(1 + f * \left(\frac{-\text{trade}_i}{\text{biggest loss}} \right) \right) \right)^{1/T}$$

But, how do these equations give you f? You find f as that value for f which maximizes either of the [1.06] or [1.07] equations (since they are all maximized at the same value for f) using a one-dimensional search. In other words, the f which is optimal is the f which maximizes either the TWR or G, the geometric mean HPR.

For example, let's assume we have two trades (i.e., $T = 2$); to be compatible with our two-to-one coin toss, we'll say that one trade lost $1,000 and one trade made $2,000. As a search technique for f, we will use the rather crude method of starting out testing an f value of .01 to 1.0 by .01. So, starting with an f of .01, we figure the HPRs. Since $T = 2$, there are only two HPRs corresponding to the two trades:

Trade	HPR
−1000	$1 + .01 * (--1000 / -1000) = 1 + .01 * -1 = .99$
2000	$1 + .01 * (-2000 / -1000) = 1 + .01 * 2 = 1.02$

Multiplying the HPRs together, we obtain the TWR of .99 * 1.02 = 1.0098. That is the TWR corresponding to an f of .01. Next we try it at .02, then .03, etc., and continue to do so until the TWR returned is less than the previous TWR. This occurs when we try an f value of .26 here, meaning that the optimal f, the peak of the curve, occurred at an f of .25.

What does it mean, though, to have an optimal f of such and such a value? We know it means to bet that percentage of your stake, but when trading markets, how many, say, futures contracts, should you put on to be betting $x\%$ of your stake?

The way to determine this, which was introduced in the 1990 book, is to divide the absolute value of the largest losing trade by this optimal f amount. The result is a dollar figure we call $f\$$:

$$f\$ = \frac{\text{abs(biggest losing trade)}}{\text{optimal } f} \qquad [1.08]$$

Thus, if we have an optimal f of .25, and our biggest losing trade is -1000, then

$$f\$ = \frac{\text{abs}(-1000)}{.25}$$

$$= \frac{1000}{.25}$$

$$= 4000$$

The $f\$$ figure is then divided into the account equity to determine how many contracts (or shares of stock) to trade. Thus, if we trade one contract for every \$4,000 in equity in the example, we are, in effect, risking 25% of our stake on each play.

This figure, our account equity divided by $f\$$, is then rounded down to the integer, since you can only make integer bets, and it is rounded down to the integer rather than up because if you are going to err, you are best off to err to the left of the peak (have on too few contracts) than to the right of the peak (having on too many contracts) of the f curve:

$$\text{Number of units to trade} = \text{int}\left(\frac{\text{account equity}}{f\$}\right) \qquad [1.09]$$

So, if we have a \$25,000 account:

$$\text{Number of units to trade} = \text{int}\left(\frac{\$25,000}{\$4,000}\right)$$

$$= \text{int}(6.25)$$

$$= 6$$

Thus, we would trade six contracts.

What is meant by a *unit?* A unit is whatever you decide. It can be one commodity contract, option contract, one share of stock, or 100 shares of stock. You must decide what a unit is going to be for the items you are trading. Then, you figure your HPRs in the context of trading one unit. That is, the dollar amounts won or lost on the trades are based on trading what you are defining as one unit. Then, the HPRs are figured, so when you finally get to Equation 1.08, the f\$, you know that you trade 1 unit for every f\$ in account equity.

Sometimes a unit can be difficult to determine. For instance, someone trading foreign exchange on the interbank market has the added problem that the size of the trade is a function of the price. Thus, for an interbank trader to determine how many units he should trade, he should always do his money management calculations based upon trading the reciprocal, as is done in the futures market, then convert back to forex.

Since the closer you can cut it in terms of unit size, the better—that is, the more expected log of wealth maximization will work for you—you should strive to keep your unit sizes as small as possible. For instance, rather than using a unit size of 100 shares, you may wish to use a unit size of one share, then deal with the odd lots when you trade. Rather than deal with full futures contracts, perhaps figure one unit as being based upon a mini contract. Thus, if it takes, say, two minis to one full contract, and your answer is to trade eleven minis, you can trade five regular contracts and one mini. Operating in this manner will make the expected log of wealth maximization work better for you than trading in huge unit sizes.

The (geometric) mathematical expectation is what you made, per unit, per trade. It is far more important than the arithmetic mathematical expectation, which is often referred to as *average trade*. The geometric mathematical expectation, the real *average trade*—real because it is what you really made per contract, per trade—is computed as:

(Geometric) Mathematical Expectation = f\$ * (Geometric mean HPR – 1)

Thus, for our two-to-one coin toss game, even though the arithmetic mathematical expectation was .50, the geometric, at the .25 f level, was:

(Geometric) Mathematical Expectation = 4 * (1.060660172 – 1)

$$= 4 * .060660172$$

$$= .242640688$$

Which is what you really would have made per unit per play (not .50) when you are making one bet for every four dollars in your stake in this two-to-one coin toss game.

When the term *the expectation* or *the edge* is referred to in the literature, it should be thought of to mean the arithmetic, not the geometric, mathematical expectation.

THE ESTIMATED GEOMETRIC MEAN (OR HOW THE DISPERSION OF OUTCOMES AFFECTS GEOMETRIC GROWTH)

This discussion will use a gambling illustration for the sake of simplicity. Let's consider two systems: system A which wins 10% of the time and has a twenty-eight-to-one win/loss ratio and system B which wins 70% of the time and has a one-to-one ratio. Our mathematical expectation, per unit bet, for A is 1.9 and for B is .4. Therefore, we can say that for every unit bet, system A will return, on average, 4.75 times as much as system B. But, let's examine this under fixed fractional trading. We can find our optimal *f*s by dividing the mathematical expectations by the win/loss ratios (per Equation [1.04b]). This gives us an optimal *f* of .0678 for A and .4 for B. The geometric means for each system at their optimal *f* levels are then:

$$A = 1.044176755$$

$$B = 1.0857629$$

System	% Wins	Win:Loss	ME	*f*	Geomean
A	.1	28:1	1.9	.0678	1.0441768
B	.7	1:1	.4	.4	1.0857629

As you can see, system B, although less than one-fourth the mathematical expectation of A, makes almost twice as much per bet (returning 8.57629% of your entire stake per bet, on average, when reinvesting at the optimal *f* levels) as does A (returning 4.4176755% of your entire stake per bet, on average, when reinvesting at the optimal *f* levels).

Now, assuming a 50% drawdown on equity will require a 100% gain to recoup, then:

1.044177 to the power of *x* is equal to 2.0 at approximately *x* equals 16.5, or more than 16 trades to recoup from a 50% drawdown for system A. Contrast this to system B where 1.0857629 to the power of *x* is equal to 2.0 at approximately *x* equals 9, or 9 trades for system B to recoup from a 50% drawdown.

What's going on here? Is this because system B has a higher percentage of winning trades? The reason B is outperforming A has to do with the dispersion of outcomes, and its effect on the growth function. Most people have the mistaken impression that the growth function, the TWR, is:

$$TWR = (1 + R)^T$$

where R = interest rate per period, e.g., 7% = .07
       T = number of periods

Since $1 + R$ is the same thing as an HPR, we can say that most people have the mistaken impression that the growth function,* the TWR, is:

$$TWR = HPR^T$$

This function is only true when the return (i.e., the HPR) is constant, which is not the case in trading.

The real growth function in trading (or any event where the HPR is not constant) is the multiplicative product of the HPRs. Assume we are trading coffee, and our optimal f is one contract for every $21,000 in equity, and we have two trades, a loss of $210 and a gain of $210, for HPRs of .99 and 1.01, respectively. In this example, our TWR would be:

$$TWR = 1.01 * .99$$

$$= .9999$$

An insight can be gained by using the estimated geometric mean (EGM), which very closely approximates the geometric mean, Equation [1.07]:

$$G = \sqrt{A^2 - S^2} \qquad\qquad [1.10a]$$

---

* Many people mistakenly use the arithmetic average HPR in the equation for HPR^T. As is demonstrated here, this will not give the true TWR after T plays. What you must use is the geometric average HPR, rather than the arithmetic in HPR^T. This will give you the true TWR. If the standard deviation in HPRs is 0, then the arithmetic average HPR and the geometric average HPR are equivalent, and it matters not which you use, arithmetic or geometric average HPR, in such a case.

or:

$$G = \sqrt{A^2 - V} \qquad [1.10b]$$

where G = geometric mean HPR
A = arithmetic mean HPR
S = standard deviation in HPRs
V = variance in HPRs

Now we take Equations [1.07] and [1.10a and b] to the power of n to estimate the TWR. This will very closely approximate the *multiplicative* growth function, the actual TWR, of Equation [1.06]:

$$\text{TWR} = \left(\sqrt{A^2 - S^2}\right)^T \qquad [1.11]$$

where T = number of periods
A = arithmetic mean HPR
S = population standard deviation in HPRs

The insight gained is that we can see, mathematically, the tradeoff between an increase in the arithmetic average trade (the HPR) versus the dispersion in the HPRs (the standard deviations or the variance); hence, the reason that the 70% one-to-one system did better than the 10% twenty-eight-to-one system.

Our goal should be to maximize the coefficient of this function, to maximize Equations [1.10a and b]: Expressed literally, to maximize *the square root of the quantity HPR squared minus the variance in HPRs.*

The exponent of the estimated TWR, T, will take care of itself. That is to say that increasing T is not a problem, as we can increase the number of markets we are following, trading more short-term types of systems, etc.

We can rewrite Equation [1.10a] to appear as:

$$A^2 = G^2 + S^2 \qquad [1.12]$$

This brings us to the point where we can envision exactly what the relationships are. Notice that this equation is the familiar Pythagorean theorem, the hypotenuse of a right-angle triangle squared equals the sum of the squares of its sides (Figure 1.6)! But here, the hypotenuse is A, and we want to maximize one of the legs, G.

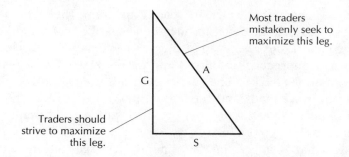

FIGURE 1.6 Pythagorean theorem in money management.

In maximizing G, any increase in S will require an increase in A to offset. When S equals zero, then A equals G, thus conforming to the misconstrued growth function $\mathrm{TWR} = (1 + R)^T$.

So, in terms of their relative effect on G, we can state that an increase in A is equal to a decrease of the same amount in S, and vice versa. Thus, any amount by which the dispersion in trades is reduced (in terms of reducing the standard deviation) is equivalent to an increase in the arithmetic average HPR. This is true regardless of whether or not you are trading at optimal f!

If a trader is trading on a fixed fractional basis, then he wants to maximize G, not necessarily A. In maximizing G, the trader should realize that the standard deviation, S, affects G in directly the same proportion as does A, per the Pythagorean theorem! Thus, when the trader reduces the standard deviation (S) of his trades, it is equivalent to an equal increase in the arithmetic average HPR (A), and vice versa!

THE FUNDAMENTAL EQUATION OF TRADING

We can glean a lot more than just how trimming the size of our losses, or reducing our dispersion in trades, improves our bottom line. Return now to Equation [1.11], the estimated TWR. Since $(X^Y)^Z = X^{(Y*Z)}$, we can further simplify the exponents in the equation, thus simplifying Equation [1.11] to:

$$\mathrm{TWR} = (A^2 - S^2)^{T/2} \qquad [1.13]$$

This last equation, the simplification for the estimated TWR, we will call the fundamental equation for trading, since it describes how the different factors, A, S, and T, affect our bottom line in trading.

There are a few things which are readily apparent. The first of these is that if A is less than or equal to one, then regardless of the other two variables, S and T, our result can be no greater than one. If A is less than one, then as T approaches infinity, A approaches zero. This means that if A is less than or equal to one (mathematical expectation less than or equal to zero since mathematical expectation $= A - 1$), we do not stand a chance at making profits. In fact, if A is less than one, it is simply a matter of time until we go broke.

Provided that A is greater than one, we can see that increasing T increases our total profits. For each increase of one trade, the coefficient is further multiplied by its square root.

Each time we can increase T by one, we increase our TWR by a factor equivalent to the square root of the coefficient (which is the geometric mean). Thus, each time a trade occurs or an HPR elapses, each time T is increased by one, the coefficient is multiplied by the geometric mean.

An important point to note about the fundamental trading equation is that it shows that if you reduce your standard deviation to a greater extent than you reduce your arithmetic average HPR, you are better off. It stands to reason, therefore, that cutting your losses short, if possible, benefits you. But the equation demonstrates that at some point you no longer benefit by cutting your losses short. That is the point where you would be getting out of too many trades with a small loss which later would have turned profitable, thus reducing your A to a greater extent than your S.

Along these same lines, reducing big winning trades can help your program if it reduces your S greater than it reduces your A. This can be accomplished, in many cases, by incorporating options into your trading program. Having an option position which goes against your position in the underlying (either by buying long an option or writing an option) can possibly help.

As you can see, the fundamental trading equation can be utilized to dictate many changes in our trading. These changes may be in the way of tightening (or loosening) our stops, setting targets, etc. These changes are the result of inefficiencies in the way we are carrying out our trading, as well as inefficiencies in our trading program or methodology.

WHY IS f OPTIMAL?

To see that f is optimal in the sense of maximizing wealth:

$$\text{since } G = \left(\prod_{i=1}^{T} \text{HPR}_i \right)^{1/T} \qquad [1.14]$$

$$\text{and} \qquad \left(\prod_{i=1}^{T} \text{HPR}_i \right)^{1/T} = \exp \left(\frac{\sum_{i=1}^{T} \ln (\text{HPR}_i)}{T} \right) \qquad [1.15]$$

Then, if one acts to maximize the geometric mean at every holding period, if the trial is sufficiently long, by applying either the weaker law of large numbers or the central limit theorem to the sum of *independent* variables (i.e., the numerator on the right side of this equation), almost certainly higher terminal wealth will result than from using any other decision rule.

Furthermore, we can also apply Rolle's theorem to the problem of the proof of f's optimality. Recall that we are defining *optimal* here as meaning that which will result in the greatest geometric growth as the number of trials increases. The TWR is the measure of average geometric growth; thus, we wish to prove that there is a value for f which results in the greatest TWR.

Rolle's theorem states that if a *continuous* function crosses a line parallel to the x axis at two points, a and b, and the function is continuous throughout the interval a,b, then there exists at least one point in the interval where the first derivative equals zero (i.e., at least one relative extremum).

Given that all functions with a positive arithmetic mathematical expectation cross the x axis twice* (the x being the f axis), at $f = 0$ and at that point to the right where f results in computed HPRs where the variance in those HPRs exceeds the difference of the arithmetic mean of those HPRs minus one, we have our a,b interval on x, respectively. Furthermore, the first derivative of the fundamental equation of trading (i.e., the estimated TWR) is continuous for all f within the interval, since f results in AHPRs and variances in those HPRs, within the interval, which are differentiable in the function in that interval; thus the func-

---

* Actually, at $f = 0$, the TWR $= 0$, and thus we cannot say that it crosses 0 to the upside here. Instead, we can say that at an f value which is an infinitesimally small amount beyond 0, the TWR crosses a line an infinitesimally small amount above 0. Likewise to the right but in reverse, the line, the f curve, the TWR, crosses this line which is an infinitesimally small amount above the x axis as it comes back down to the x axis.

tion, the estimated TWR, is continuous within the interval. Per Rolle's theorem, it must, therefore, have at least one relative extremum in the interval, and since the interval is positive, i.e., above the x axis, the interval must contain at least one maximum.

In fact, there can be only one maximum in the interval given that the change in the geometric mean HPR (a transformation of the TWR, given that the geometric mean HPR is the Tth root of the TWR) is a direct function of the change in the AHPR and the variance, both of which vary in *opposite directions to each other as f varies,* per the Pythagorean theorem. This guarantees that there can be only one peak. Thus, there must be a peak in the interval, and there can be only one peak. There is an f which is optimal at only one value for f, where the first derivative of the TWR with respect to f equals zero.

Let us go back to Equation [1.06]. Now, we again consider our two-to-one coin toss. There are two trades, two possible scenarios. If we take the first derivative of [1.06] with respect to f, we obtain:

$$\frac{d\text{TWR}}{df} = \left(\left(1 + f * \left(\frac{-\text{trade}_1}{\text{biggest loss}}\right)\right) * \left(\frac{-\text{trade}_2}{\text{biggest loss}}\right)\right)$$

$$+ \left(\left(\frac{-\text{trade}_1}{\text{biggest loss}}\right) * \left(1 + f * \left(\frac{-\text{trade}_2}{\text{biggest loss}}\right)\right)\right) \quad [1.16]$$

If there were more than two trades, the same basic form could be used, only it would grow monstrously large in short order, so we'll use only two trades for the sake of simplicity. Thus, for the sequence $+2, -1$ at $f = .25$:

$$\frac{d\text{TWR}}{df} = \left(\left(1 + .25 * \left(\frac{-2}{-1}\right)\right) * \left(\frac{--1}{-1}\right)\right) + \left(\left(\frac{-2}{-1}\right) * \left(1 + .25 * \left(\frac{--1}{-1}\right)\right)\right)$$

$$\frac{d\text{TWR}}{df} = ((1 + .25 * 2) * -1) + (2 * (1 + .25 * -1))$$

$$\frac{d\text{TWR}}{df} = ((1 + .5) * -1) + (2 * (1 - .25))$$

$$\frac{d\text{TWR}}{df} = (1.5 * -1) + (2 * .75)$$

$$\frac{d\text{TWR}}{df} = -1.5 + 1.5 = 0$$

And we see that the function peaks at .25, where the slope of the tangent is zero, exactly at the optimal f, and no other local extremum can exist because of the restriction caused by the Pythagorean theorem.

Lastly, we will see that optimal f is indifferent to T. We can take the first derivative of the estimated TWR, Equation [1.13] with respect to T as:

$$\frac{d\text{TWR}}{dT} = (A^2 - S^2)^{T/2} * \ln (A^2 - S^2) \qquad [1.17]$$

Since $\ln(1) = 0$, then if $A^2 - S^2 = 1$, i.e., $A^2 - 1 = S^2$ (or variance), the function peaks out and the single optimal maximum TWR is found with respect to f. Notice, though, that both A, the arithmetic average HPR, and S, the standard deviation in those HPRs, are not functions of T. Instead, they are indifferent to T; thus, [1.13] is indifferent to T at the optimal f. The f which is optimal in the sense of maximizing the estimated TWR will always be the same value regardless of T.

THEY DON'T LIKE IT

Shortly after the 1990 publication of these formulas, others jumped in with the idea of finding the optimal f via a Monte Carlo simulation. One of the big criticisms the 1990 formulas received was that they didn't acknowledge the fact that you must trade in integer contract sizes; i.e., you cannot trade .37 of a gold contract. The Monte Carlo approach allowed you to determine an optimal f value given the real-world constraint of integer contract trading.

The way a Monte Carlo simulation like this might work is as follows: Assume you have a starting stake of, say, $50,000. Now, take all of the trades and throw them into a bag. Pull them out one at a time. Each time you pull one out, figure your new stake based on the f value you are presently testing. By doing this over and over, you will be able to determine that the f that was optimal was the one that had you finish with the most money.

All of that is fine and well. However, the method first presented in 1990 will give you the optimal f for the universe of starting stakes. That is, it gives the optimal f considering all possible starting stakes. Secondly, as the size of the starting stake increases, the two techniques, the 1990 formulas and the Monte Carlo approach, converge on the same value for optimal *f*. Thirdly, the smaller an integer size was, the closer the two approaches converged. That is, the smaller the unit sizes you could trade in, i.e., the closer to noninteger bets you could go, the more the two techniques converged *and* the better either technique would work. That is, the more frequently you can adjust the integer amounts you are trading in with respect to a change in equity, the more maximizing the expected value of the logarithm of capital would work in your favor. Therefore, arguably, one might be better off trading oats than S&Ps.

Finally, you need not use raw dollar amounts in figuring your HPRs in any of these calculations.* You could simply convert the trades, or outcomes over the holding periods, to percentages, use the biggest losing percentage in determining HPRs, and find what your optimal *f* was on the percentage outcomes. Then, when you go to employ Equation [1.08] for the biggest losing trade, simply take what you have been using for the biggest losing percentage, multiply that by the current price of the item, and use that as the biggest losing trade. This is shown as the following equation:

$$f\$ = \frac{\text{abs(biggest losing percentage} * \text{current price)}}{\text{optimal } f} \qquad [1.18]$$

INTRODUCTION TO PORTFOLIOS WITH OPTIMAL *f*

The 1990 book also showed a way to determine the optimal *f* values for components in a portfolio.

To begin with, whenever we are working with components in a portfolio, we must use uniform holding periods. That is, no longer can a holding period be referred to as a trade, but rather it must be a uniform length of time—a day, week, month, quarter, or year. I opt to use days, but there is no requirement that you do so. The only requirement is that you use a uniform length of time in determining HPRs, and that length is the same from one market to the next, from one trading approach to the next. Therefore, if your holding period length is, say, one day, then you determine HPRs based on the change in equity of trading one unit over one day.

---

* For more on this, see Ralph Vince, "Equalizing Optimal f," *The Mathematics of Money Management,* pp. 83–89.

The only other change to making the 1990 formulas applicable to a portfolio is simply an amendment to equation [1.05] to accommodate more than one component:

$$\text{HPR}_k = 1 + \left(\sum_{i=1}^{n} f_i * \left(\frac{-\text{trade}_{i,k}}{\text{biggest loss}} \right) \right) \tag{1.19}$$

where HPR_k = HPR for the kth holding period
             $\text{trade}_{i,k}$ = the change in equity for trading 1 unit for compo-
                 nent i over the kth period
   biggest loss = most negative change in equity for this compo-
                 nent on a one-unit basis over all holding periods
             n = number of components in the portfolio
             f_i = f associated with the ith component

Thus, you must find the n optimal f values, one for each component. Also, note that any of the f values, although they cannot be less than zero, can also be greater than one. This is so because, if there is a high enough negative correlation between two components, their f values will approach infinity.

To see this, consider two streams of outcomes. One makes two dollars over the first holding period, then loses one dollar on the second. The other stream loses $1.10 on the first holding period, but makes one dollar on the second:

Holding Period #	Stream 1	Stream 2
1	2	−1.1
2	−1	1

Notice that you can optimally assign f values of infinity to these two streams (thus, $f\$$ would be infinitely small, and you would have on infinitely many units) since, on balance, there is not a losing holding period. Notice, too, that this is far more aggressive than simply trading Stream 1 alone, which would have an optimal f of .25. Finally, notice that Stream 2 has a negative arithmetic mathematical expectation, yet, because of its negative correlation to Stream 1, you should trade an infinitely high number of units when traded together! In other words, it is possible that a negative expectation component will improve the overall performance of the portfolio by its inclusion.

The technique in the 1990 book was empirical; that is, it used the actual data itself to determine a portfolio. The 1992 book showed a way to meld the notion of optimal f for the components of a portfolio within the E-V model framework. Both methods, the 1990 empirical method and the 1992 E-V method, have their shortcomings. These shortcomings are so great that I wrote this book.

One last thing needs to be mentioned about portfolios before we continue. Suppose we have a $50,000 account, and we have a portfolio with two components. The optimal allocations, the optimal f\$ for the components, are $5,000 and $10,000, respectively. How then do we divide the $50,000 account among these two components' f\$?

The answer is very simple. First, you divide the full $50,000 by the first component's f\$. Thus, 50,000/5,000 gives 10. Thus we trade ten units of the first component. Second, take the same equity, the 50,000, and again divide by the f\$ of the next component. Thus, 50,000/10,000 gives 5. We would therefore trade five units of the second component. Note that with portfolios, your f\$ for each of the components are divided into the same account equity—there is an element of overlap of the equity—and it is the correct way to determine the number of contracts (Equation [1.09] when doing portfolios.*

FALLACIOUS NOTIONS REGARDING BOTH DRAWDOWNS AND DIVERSIFICATION

One quickly realizes that the better a trading approach appears when traded on a one-unit basis, the higher the optimal f is. Hence, the lower the f\$, the greater the quantity that will be called for. There is a paradox here. Note that the lowest the drawdown can be in terms of percentage equity retracement, when trading at any value for f (and we are all at some value for f), is f%. That is, if, for example, in our two-to-one coin toss game, we see we have an optimal f of .25, or we make one bet for every four dollars in account equity (the f\$), then as soon as the largest losing bet or trade is hit (−$1 in this case), we will be down f%. As soon as we see a loss, we will have retraced f% of our equity.

---

* For more on this, see Ralph Vince, "One Combined Bankroll Versus Separate Bankrolls," *The Mathematics of Money Management,* New York: Wiley, 1992, pp. 68–70.

This is true not only at the optimal f level, but at any f level. Again, assume our two-to-one coin toss game, but assume we are trading at the level of an f of .1, which means we make one bet for every ten dollars in account equity. As soon as the largest losing bet or trade is hit, we will be down 10% on our equity. This presents a great paradox in that the better a system, the greater the drawdown, since you will be inclined to trade it at a higher f level!

It would appear on the surface, then, that in our two-to-one coin toss game it makes little difference whether we trade at the .1 level for f, which, after 40 plays saw a 366% gain with at least a 10% drawdown, or the .25 optimal which saw a 955% return with at least a 25% drawdown. It looks like six of one and one-half dozen of the other. However, if we extrapolate this out to 100 plays, the expected minimum drawdowns stay the same, yet the expected gains go to 4,590% at $f = .1$ vs. 36,009% at $f = .25$. Clearly, the difference in the ratio of gain to expected minimum equity retracement is greatest at optimal f than any other f value, and the difference grows as more holding periods are encountered.

Notice that expected minimum equity retracement changes arithmetically, whereas the gain changes exponentially with respect to f. Thus, we can state that *when you dilute f (trade lesser quantity than is optimal)* you reduce drawdowns arithmetically, while you also reduce returns exponentially. Now, going to the right of the peak reduces only returns (again exponentially), while it increases minimum expected drawdown (in terms of percentage equity retracements again) arithmetically.

There are also some misguided notions which must be addressed at this time regarding diversification. The real benefit of diversification is not that it provides safety, as some people mistakenly (and intuitively) believe. Rather, the real benefit of diversification is expressed mathematically in the fundamental equation of trading. *Diversification lets you get more T off in a given period of time. Thus, it provides for greater growth in the given time period. It does not provide for added safety.*

Furthermore, by diversifying, you add more dimensions to the landscape, thus making it even more treacherous and more likely for ruin. Regardless of how many components a portfolio has, there will come a time where everything has a bad day together. Thus, adding more components may smooth out the equity curve (thus giving the misguided notion of providing for safety), but will frequently increase worst-case drawdown as well!

Also, regarding the conventional notion (again misguided) that more components hinder performance or that the marginal benefit from each increase in components diminishes, i.e., reaches an asymptote. On the contrary, the line is not logarithmic, but rather goes up and to the right in a straight line since all we are doing through diversification is increasing T. Each increase in T increases growth equivalently, and this does not reach an asymptote.

THE NEXT STEP

The real problem with these formulas [1.05 to 1.07] was that they made the assumption that all HPRs had an equal probability of occurrence. What was needed was a new formula that allowed for different probabilities associated with different HPRs. Such a formula would allow you to find an optimal f given a description of a probability distribution of HPRs. Two years later, in 1992, I published[9] a set of formulas which did exactly that:

$$\text{HPR} = \left(1 + \left(\frac{A}{\left(\frac{W}{f}\right)}\right)\right)^{P} \qquad [1.20]$$

where A = outcome of the scenario
P = probability of the scenario
W = worst outcome of all n scenarios
f = value for f which we are testing

Now, we obtain the terminal wealth relative, or TWR*:

$$\text{TWR} = \prod_{i=1}^{T} \text{HPR}_i \qquad [1.21]$$

---

* In this formulation, unlike the 1990 formulations, the TWR has no special meaning. In this instance, it is simply an interim value used to find G, and it does *not* represent the multiple made on our starting stake.

or

$$\text{TWR} = \prod_{i=1}^{T} \left(1 + \left(\frac{A_i}{\left(\frac{W}{f}\right)} \right) \right)^{P_i}$$

Finally, if we take Equation [1.21] to the Σp_i root, we can find our average compound growth per play, also called the geometric mean HPR, which will become more important later on:

$$G = \text{TWR}^{1/\Sigma p_i} \qquad\qquad [1.22]$$

or

$$G = \left(\prod_{i=1}^{T} \left(\left(1 + \left(\frac{A_i}{\left(\frac{W}{f}\right)} \right) \right)^{P_i} \right) \right)^{1/\Sigma p_i}$$

where T = number of different scenarios
           TWR = terminal wealth relative
           HPR_i = holding period return of the ith scenario
           A_i = outcome of the ith scenario
           P_i = probability of the ith scenario
           W = worst outcome of all n scenarios
           f = value for f which we are testing

Just as you could use Equation(s) [1.04] to solve Equation(s) [1.03], likewise you can use Equation [1.22] to solve *any* optimal f problem. You can use Equation [1.22] in lieu of Equations [1.03 to 1.07]. It will yield the same answers as the Kelly formulas when the data correctly has a Bernoulli distribution. It will yield the same answers as the 1990 formulas if you pump a distribution of trades through it (where the probability of each trade is $1/T$). This formula can be used to maximize the expected value of the logarithm of any starting quantity of anything when there is exponential growth involved. We will now see how to employ this formula in the context of *scenario planning*.

SCENARIO PLANNING

People who forecast for a living, be they economists, stock market fore-casters, meteorologists, government agencies, etc., have a notorious his-tory for incorrect forecasts. Most decisions anyone must make in life usually require that the individual make a forecast about the future.

There are a couple of pitfalls that immediately crop up. To begin with, people generally make more optimistic assumptions about the future than the actual probabilities. Most people feel that they are far more likely to win the lottery this month than they are to die in an auto acci-dent, even though the probabilities of the latter are greater. This is not true only on the level of the individual, it is even more pronounced at the group level. When people work together, they tend to see a favor-able outcome as the most likely result.

The second pitfall—and the more harmful—is that people make straight-line forecasts into the future. People predict what the price of a gallon of gas will be two years from now; they predict what will happen with their jobs, who will be the next president, what the next styles will be, and on and on. Whenever we think of the future, we tend to think in terms of a single most likely outcome. As a result, whenever we must make decisions, whether as an individual or a group, we tend to make these decisions based on what we think will be the single most likely outcome in the future. As a consequence, we are extremely vulnerable to unpleasant surprises.

Scenario planning is a partial solution to this problem. A scenario is simply a possible forecast, a story about one way that the future might unfold. Scenario planning is a collection of scenarios, to cover the spec-trum of possibilities. Of course, the complete spectrum can never be cov-ered, but the scenario planner wants to cover as many possibilities as he or she can. By acting in this manner, as opposed to using a straight-line forecast of the most likely outcome, the scenario planner can prepare for the future as it unfolds. Furthermore, scenario planning allows the plan-ner to be prepared for what might otherwise be an unexpected event. Scenario planning is tuned to reality in that it recognizes that *certainty is an illusion.*

Suppose you are in a position where you are involved in the long-run planning for your company. Let's say you make a particular product. Rather than making a single most likely straight-line forecast, you decide to exercise scenario planning. You will need to sit down with the other planners and brainstorm for possible scenarios. What if you cannot get enough of the raw materials to make your product? What if one of your competitors fails? What if a new competitor emerges? What if you have severely underestimated demand for this product? What if a war breaks out on such and such a continent? What if it is a nuclear war?

Because each scenario is only one of several possible, each scenario can be considered seriously. But what do you do once you have defined these scenarios?

To begin with, you must determine what goal you would like to achieve for each given scenario. Depending upon the scenario, the goal need not be a positive one. For instance, under a bleak scenario, your goal may simply be damage control. Once you have defined a goal for a given scenario, you then need to draw up the contingency plans pertaining to that scenario to achieve the desired goal. For instance, in the rather unlikely bleak scenario where your goal is damage control, you need to have plans to go to should this scenario manifest itself so that you can minimize the damage. Scenario planning, above all else, provides the planner with a course of action to take should a certain scenario develop. It forces you to make plans before the fact; it forces you to be prepared for the unexpected.

Scenario planning, however, can do a lot more. There is a hand-in-glove fit between scenario planning and optimal f. Optimal f allows us to determine the optimal quantity to allocate to a given set of possible scenarios. Our existence limits us to existing in only one scenario at a time, even though we are planning for multiple futures, multiple scenarios. Therefore, oftentimes, scenario planning puts us in a position where we must make a decision regarding how much of a resource to allocate today, given the possible scenarios of tomorrow. This is the true heart of scenario planning: quantifying it.

First, we must define each unique scenario. Second, we must assign a probability of that scenario's occurrence. Being a probability means that this number is between 0 and 1. We need not consider any further scenarios with a probability of 0. Note that these probabilities are not cumulative. In other words, the probability assigned to a given scenario is unique to that scenario. Suppose we are decision makers for XYZ Manufacturing Corporation. Two of the many scenarios we have are as follows. In one scenario, we have the probability of XYZ Manufacturing filing for bankruptcy with a probability of .15, and, in another scenario, we have XYZ being put out of business by intense foreign competition with a probability of .07. Now, we must ask if the first scenario, filing for bankruptcy, includes filing for bankruptcy due to the second scenario, intense foreign competition. If it does, then the probabilities in the first scenario must not take the probabilities of the second scenario into account, and we must amend the probabilities of the first scenario to be .08 (.15 − .07).

Just as important as the uniqueness of each probability to each scenario is that the sum of the probabilities of all of the scenarios we are considering must equal 1 exactly. They must equal not 1.01 nor .99, but 1.

For each scenario, we now have a probability of just that scenario assigned. We must now also assign an outcome result. This is a numerical value. It can be dollars made or lost as a result of a scenario manifesting itself; it can be units of utility or medication or anything. However, our output is going to be in the same units that we put in.

You must have at least one scenario with a negative outcome in order to use this technique. This is mandatory.

A last prerequisite to using this technique is that the arithmetic mathematical expectation the sum of all of the outcome results times their respective probabilities, (Equation [1.01a]), must be greater than zero. If the arithmetic mathematical expectation equals zero or is negative, the following technique cannot be used.* That is not to say that scenario planning itself cannot be used. It can and should. However, optimal f can only be incorporated with scenario planning when there is a positive mathematical expectation.

Lastly, you must try to cover as much of the spectrum of outcomes as possible. In other words, you really want to account for 99% of the possible outcomes. This may sound nearly impossible, but many scenarios can be made broader so that you don't need 10,000 scenarios to cover 99% of the spectrum.

In making your scenarios broader, you must avoid the common pitfall of three scenarios: an optimistic one, a pessimistic one, and a third in which things remain the same. This is too simple, and the answers derived therefrom are often too crude to be of any value. Would you want to find your optimal f for a trading system based on only three trades?

So, even though there may be an unknowably large number of scenarios to cover the entire spectrum, we can cover what we believe to be

---

* However, later in the text we will be using scenario planning for portfolios, and, therein, a negative arithmetic mathematical expectation will be allowed, and can possibly benefit the portfolio as a whole.

about 99% of the spectrum of outcomes. If this makes for an unmanageably large number of scenarios, we can make the scenarios broader to trim down their number. However, by trimming down their number, we lose a certain amount of information. When we trim down the number of scenarios (by broadening them) to only three (a common pitfall), we have effectively eliminated so much information that the effectiveness of this technique is severely hampered.

What, then, is a good number of scenarios to have? As many as you can and still manage them. Here, a computer is a great asset.

Think of the two-to-one coin toss as a spectrum of two scenarios. Each has a probability, and that probability is .5 for each scenario, labeled heads and tails. Each has an outcome, +2 and −1, respectively:

Scenario	Probability	Outcome
Heads	.5	2
Tails	.5	−1

Assume again that we are decision making for XYZ. We are looking at marketing a new product of ours in a primitive, remote little country. Assume we have five possible scenarios we are looking at (in reality, you would have many more than this, but we'll use five for the sake of simplicity). These five scenarios portray what we perceive as possible futures for this primitive remote country, their probabilities of occurrence, and the gain or loss of investing there.

Scenario	Probability	Result
War	.1	−$500,000
Trouble	.2	−$200,000
Stagnation	.2	0
Peace	.45	$500,000
Prosperity	.05	$1,000,000
	Sum 1.00	

The sum of our probabilities equals 1. We have at least one scenario with a negative result, and our mathematical expectation is positive:

$$(.1 * -500,000) + (.2 * -200,000) + \ldots \text{etc.} = 185,000$$

We can, therefore, use the technique on this set of scenarios.

Notice first, however, that if we used the single most likely outcome method, we would conclude that peace will be the future of this country, and we would then act as though peace were to occur, as though it were a certainty, only vaguely remaining aware of the other possibilities.

Returning to the technique, we must determine the optimal f. The optimal f is that value for f (between zero and one) which maximizes the geometric mean, using Equations [1.20 to 1.22]. Now, we obtain the terminal wealth relative, or TWR,* using Equation [1.21]. Finally, if we take Equation [1.21] to the Σp_i root, we can find our average compound growth per play, also called the geometric mean HPR, which will become more important later on. We use Equation [1.22] for this.

Here is how to perform these equations. To begin with, we must decide on an optimization scheme, a way of searching through the f values to find that f which maximizes our equation. Again, we can do this with a straight loop with f from .01 to 1, through iteration, or through parabolic interpolation.

Next, we must determine the worst possible result for a scenario among all of the scenarios we are looking at, regardless of how small the probability of that scenario's occurrence are. In the example of XYZ Corporation, this is –$500,000.

Now, for each possible scenario, we must first divide the worst possible outcome by negative f. In our XYZ Corporation example, we will assume that we are going to loop through f values from .01 to 1. Therefore, we start out with an f value of .01. Now, if we divide the worst possible outcome of the scenarios under consideration by the negative value for f, we get the following:

$$\frac{-\$500,000}{-.01} = 50,000,000$$

Notice how negative values divided by negative values yield positive results, and vice versa. Therefore, our result in this case is positive. Now, as we go through each scenario, we will divide the outcome of the scenario by the result just obtained. Since the outcome to the first scenario is also the worst scenario—a loss of $500,000—we now have:

$$\frac{-\$500,000}{50,000,000} = -.01$$

---

* In this formulation, unlike the 1990 formulations, the TWR has no special meaning. In this instance, it is simply an interim value used to find G, and it does *not* represent the multiple made on our starting stake.

The next step is to add this value to 1. This gives us:

$$1 + (-.01) = .99$$

Last, we take this answer to the power of the probability of its occurrence, which in our example is .1:

$$.99 \wedge .1 = .9989954713$$

Next, we go to the next scenario labeled *Trouble,* where there is a .2 loss of $200,000. Our worst-case result is still –$500,000. The *f* value we are working on is still .01, so the value we want to divide this scenario's result by is still 50 million:

$$\frac{-200,000}{50,000,000} = -.004$$

Working through the rest of the steps to obtain our HPR:

$$1 + (-.004) = .996$$

$$.996 \wedge .2 = .9991987169$$

If we continue through the scenarios for this test value of .01 for *f,* we will find the three HPRs corresponding to the last three scenarios:

Stagnation	1.0
Peace	1.004487689
Prosperity	1.000990622

Once we have turned each scenario into an HPR for the given *f* value, we must multiply these HPRs together:

$$
\begin{array}{r}
.9989954713 \\
*\quad .9991987169 \\
*\ 1.0 \\
*\ 1.004487689 \\
*\ 1.000990622 \\
\hline
1.003667853
\end{array}
$$

This gives us the interim TWR, which in this case is 1.003667853. Our next step is to take this to the power of 1 divided by the sum of the probabilities. Since the sum of the probabilities will always equal 1 the way we are calculating this, we can state that we must raise the TWR to the power of 1 to give us the geometric mean. Since anything raised to the power of 1 equals itself, we can say that, in this case, our geometric mean equals the TWR. We therefore have a geometric mean of 1.003667853.

If, however, we relaxed the constraint that each scenario must have a unique probability, then we could allow the sum of the probabilities of the scenarios to be greater than 1. In such a case, we would have to raise our TWR to the power of 1 divided by this sum of the probabilities, in order to derive the geometric mean.

The answer we have just obtained in our example is our geometric mean corresponding to an f value of .01. Now we move on to an f value of .02, and repeat the whole process until we have found the geometric mean corresponding to an f value of .02. We will proceed as such until we arrive at that value for f which yields the highest geometric mean.

In the case of our example, we find that the highest geometric mean is obtained at an f value of .57, which yields a geometric mean of 1.1106. Dividing our worst possible outcome to a scenario (−500,000) by the negative optimal f yields a result of $877,192.35. In other words, if XYZ Corporation wants to commit to marketing this new product in this remote country, they will optimally commit this amount to this venture at this time. As time goes by and things develop, the scenarios, their resultant outcomes, and probabilities will likewise change. This f amount will then change as well. The more XYZ Corporation keeps abreast of these changing scenarios, as well as the more accurate the scenarios they develop as input are, the more accurate their decisions will be. Note that if XYZ Corporation cannot commit this $877,192.35 to this undertaking at this time, then they are too far beyond the peak of the f curve. It is the equivalent of the guy who has too many commodity contracts with respect to what the optimal f says he should have. If XYZ Corporation commits more than this amount to this project at this time, the situation would be analogous to a commodity trader with too few contracts.

There is an important point to note about scenarios and trading. What you use for a scenario can be any of a number of things:

1. It can be, as in the previous example, the outcomes that a given trade may take. This is useful if you are trading only one item. However, when you trade a portfolio of items, you violate the rule that all holding period lengths must be uniform.

2. If you know what the distribution of price outcomes will be, you can use that for scenarios. For example, suppose you have reason to believe that prices for the next day for a given item are normally distributed. Therefore, you can discern your scenarios based on the normal distribution. For example, in the normal distribution, 97.72% of the time, prices will not exceed two standard deviations to the upside, and 99.86% of the time they will not exceed three standard deviations to the upside. Therefore, as one scenario, you can have as the result something between two to three standard deviations in price to the upside (whatever dollar amount that would be to you trading one unit over the next day, holding period), whose probability would be .9986 − .9772 = .0214, or 2.14% probability.

3. You can use the distributions of possible monetary outcomes for trading one unit with the given market approach over the next holding period. This is my preferred method, and it lends itself well to portfolio construction under the new framework.

Although I strongly recommend using the third item from the preceding list, whichever method you use, remember that *you want to be constantly updating your scenarios, their outcomes, and the probability of occurrences as conditions change. Then, you always want to go into the next holding period with what the formulas presently tell you is optimal.** The situation is analogous to that of a blackjack player. As the composition of the deck changes with each card drawn, so, too, do the player's probabilities. However, he must always adjust to what the probabilities currently dictate.

Although the quantity discussed here is a quantity of money, it can be a quantity of anything and the technique is just as valid.

If you create different scenarios for the stock market, the optimal f derived from this methodology will give you the correct percentage to be invested in the stock market at any given time. For instance, if the f returned is .65, then that means that 65% of your equity should be in the stock market with the remaining 35% in, say, cash. This approach will provide you with the greatest geometric growth of your capital in a long-

---

* For more on this, see Vince, "Treat Each Play as if Infinitely Repeated," *The Mathematics of Money Management,* pp. 71–73.

run sense. Of course, again, the output is only as accurate as the input you have provided the system with in terms of scenarios, their probabilities of occurrence, and resultant payoffs and costs.

This same process can be used as an alternative parametric technique for determining the optimal f for a given trade. Suppose you are making your trading decisions based on fundamentals. You could, if you wanted, outline the different scenarios that the trade may take. The more scenarios, and the more accurate the scenarios, the more accurate your results would be. Let's say you are looking to buy a municipal bond for income, but you're not planning on holding the bond to maturity. You could outline numerous different scenarios of how the future might unfold. Now, you can use these scenarios to determine how much to invest in this particular bond issue.

Suppose a trader is presented with a decision to buy soybeans. He may be using Elliot Wave, he may be using weather forecasts, but whatever he is using, let's say he can discern the following scenarios for this potential trade:

Scenario	Probability	Result
Best-case outcome	.05	150/cent bushel (profit)
Quite likely	.4	10/cent bushel (profit)
Typical	.45	−5/cent bushel (loss)
Not good	.05	−30/cent bushel (loss)
Disastrous	.05	−150/cent bushel (loss)

Now, when our Elliot Wave soybean trader (or weather forecaster soybean trader) paints this set of scenarios, this set of possible outcomes to this trade, and, in order to maximize his long-run growth (and survival), assumes that he must make this same trading decision an infinite number of times into the future, he will find, using this scenario planning approach, that optimally he should bet .02 (2%) of his stake on this trade. This translates into putting on one soybean contract for every $375,000 in equity, since the scenario with the largest loss, −150/cent bushel, divided by the optimal f for this scenario set, .02, results in $7,500/.02 = $375,000. Thus, at one contract for every $375,000 in equity, the trader can be said to be risking 2% of his stake on the next trade.

For each trade, regardless of the basis the trader uses for making the trade (i.e., Elliot Wave, weather, etc.), the scenario parameters may change. Yet the trader must maximize the long run geometric growth of his account by assuming that the same scenario parameters will be infinitely repeated. Otherwise, the trader pays a severe price, as was discussed with reference to Figure 1.2. Notice in our soybean trader example, if the trader were to go *to the right of the peak of the* f *curve* (that is, have slightly too many contracts), he gains no benefit. In other words, if our soybean trader were to put on one contract for every $300,000 in account equity, he would actually make less money in the long run than putting on one contract for every $375,000.

When we are presented with a decision with which there is a different set of scenarios for each facet of the decision, selecting the scenario whose geometric mean corresponding to its optimal f is greatest will maximize our decision in an asymptotic sense.

For example, suppose we are presented with a decision that involves two possible choices. It could have many possible choices, but for the sake of simplicity we will say it has two possible choices, which we will call "white" and "black". If we choose the decision labeled white, we determine that it will present the possible future scenarios to us:

White decision:

Scenario	Probability	Result
A	.3	−20
B	.4	0
C	.3	30

Mathematical expectation = $3.00
Optimal f = .17
Geometric mean = 1.0123

It doesn't matter what these scenarios are, they can be anything. To further illustrate this, they will simply be assigned letters, A, B, C in this discussion. Further, it doesn't matter what the result is; it can be just about anything.

Our analysis determines that the black decision will present the following scenarios:

Black decision:

Scenario	Probability	Result
A	.3	−10
B	.4	5
C	.15	6
D	.15	20

Mathematical expectation = $2.90
Optimal f = .31
Geometric mean = 1.0453

Many people would opt for the white decision, since it is the decision with the higher mathematical expectation. With the white decision, you can expect, *on average,* a $3.00 gain versus black's $2.90 gain. Yet the black decision is actually the correct decision because it results in a greater geometric mean. With the black decision, you would expect to make 4.53% (1.0453 − 1) *on average* as opposed to white's 1.23% gain. When you consider the effects of reinvestment, the black decision makes more than three times as much, on average, as does the white decision!

The reader may protest at this point that, "We're not doing this thing over again; we're only doing it once. We're not reinvesting back into the same future scenarios here. Won't we come out ahead if we always select the highest arithmetic mathematical expectation for each set of decisions that present themselves to us?"

The only time we want to be making decisions based on greatest arithmetic mathematical expectation is if we are planning on not reinvesting the money risked on the decision at hand. Since, in almost every case, the money risked on an event today will be risked again on a different event in the future, and money made or lost in the past effects what we have available to risk today, we should decide, based on geometric mean, to maximize the long-run growth of our money. Even though the scenarios that present themselves tomorrow won't be the same as those today, by always deciding based on greatest geometric mean, we are maximizing our decisions. It is analogous to a dependent trials process, like a game of blackjack. In each hand, the probabilities change and, therefore, the optimal fraction to bet changes as well. By always betting what is optimal for that hand, however, we maximize our long-run growth. Remember that, to maximize long-run growth, we must look at the current contest as one that expands infinitely into the future. In other words, we must look at each individual event as though we were to play it an infinite number of times if we wanted to maximize growth over many plays of different contests.

As a generalization, whenever the outcome of an event has an effect on the outcome(s) of subsequent event(s), we are better off to maximize for greatest geometric expectation. In the rare cases where the outcome of an event has no effect on subsequent events, we are then better off to maximize for greatest arithmetic expectation.

Mathematical expectation (arithmetic) does not take the dispersion between the outcomes of the different scenarios into account, and, therefore, can lead to incorrect decisions when reinvestment is considered.

Using this method of scenario planning gets you quantitatively positioned with respect to the possible scenarios, their outcomes, and the likelihood of their occurrence. The method is inherently more conservative than positioning yourself per the greatest arithmetic mathematical expectation. The geometric mean of a data set is never greater than the arithmetic mean. Likewise, this method can never have you position yourself (have a greater commitment) otherwise than selecting by the greatest arithmetic mathematical expectation would. In the asymptotic sense (the long-run sense), this is not only the superior method of positioning yourself as it achieves greatest geometric growth, it is also a more conservative one than positioning yourself per the greatest arithmetic mathematical expectation.

Since reinvestment is almost always a fact of life (except on the day before you retire)—that is, you reuse the money that you are using today—we must make today's decision under the assumption that the same decision will present itself a thousand times over, in order to maximize the results of our decision. We must make our decisions and position ourselves in order to maximize geometric expectation. Further, since the outcomes of most events do, in fact, have an effect on the outcomes of subsequent events, we should make our decisions and position ourselves based on maximum geometric expectation. This tends to lead to decisions and positions which are not always obvious.

SCENARIO SPECTRUMS

We now must become familiar with the notion of a *scenario spectrum*. A scenario spectrum is a set of scenarios, aligned in succession, left to right, from worst outcome towards best, which range in probability from 0% to 100%. For example, consider the scenario spectrum for a simple coin toss whereby we lose on heads and win on tails, and both have a .5 probability of occurrence (Figure 1.7).

A scenario spectrum can have more than two scenarios—you can have as many scenarios as you like. (See Figure 1.8.)

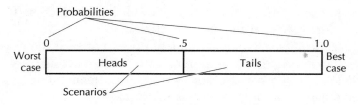

FIGURE 1.7

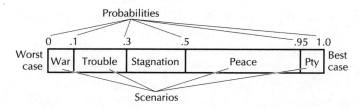

FIGURE 1.8

This scenario spectrum corresponds to the following scenarios, taken from the previous section pertaining to **XYZ** Manufacturing Corporation's assessment of marketing a new product in a remote little country:

Scenario	Probability	Result	Prob × Result
War	.1	−$500,000	−$50,000
Trouble	.2	−$200,000	−$40,000
Stagnation	.2	$0	$0
Peace	.45	$500,000	$225,000
Prosperity	.05	$1,000,000	$50,000
Sum	1.00	Expectation	$185,000

Notice that this is a *valid scenario spectrum* since:

A. There is at least one scenario with a negative result.
B. The sum of the probabilities equals 1.00.
C. The scenarios within the spectrum do not overlap.

For example the stagnation scenario implies peace. However, the stagnation scenario implies peace with zero economic growth. The peace scenario is separate and apart from this, and implies peace with at least some economic growth. In other words, the stagnation scenario is *not* encapsulated in the peace scenario, nor is any scenario encapsulated in another.

One last point about scenario spectrums, and this is very important. All scenarios within a given spectrum must pertain to outcomes of a given holding period. Again, the length of the holding period can be any length you choose—it can be one day, one week, quarter, month, year, whatever, but the holding period must be decided upon. Once decided upon, all scenarios in a given spectrum must pertain to possible outcomes over the *next* holding period, and all scenario spectrums must be for the same length holding period. This is critical. Thus, if you decide upon one day for the holding period length, then all of your scenarios in all of your scenario spectrums must pertain to possible outcomes for the next day.

Later in this text we will see how to determine optimal allocations to various scenario spectrums, all being traded simultaneously. This is an outgrowth of my earlier work of optimal f and options. As a prerequisite, we must learn about conditional probabilities. Before that, however, there is still some preliminary material to cover.

ADDENDUM ONE

Deficit Reduction Through *Increased* Gross Domestic Product Variance

The March 25, 1993, *Wall Street Journal* contained a particularly interesting editorial by W. Kurt Hauser. In a nutshell, perhaps unfairly to Mr. Hauser, the editorial stated that regardless of tax rates and tax code changes in the postwar period, the percentage of GDP collected in taxes (in the United States) has consistently averaged 19.5%. Further, the variance about this 19.5% average has been relatively small, the extremes being 21.1% on the high end (1981) and 17.9% on the low end (1964 and 1965). Mr. Hauser presented a very convincing case that GDP must grow at a faster rate than government expenditures. This implies that the 1993 Clinton tax proposal is flawed in that lower taxes are more stimulative to GDP, not higher taxes as called for by the Clinton proposals.

According to Mr. Hauser, the road to deficit reduction lies not in increasing tax rates, but rather in increasing GDP. Further, this seems to be a widely held notion. However, deficit reduction can also be achieved by increasing the *variance* in GDP, just as effectively as an increase in GDP itself! This notion flies in the face, not only of conventional thinking, but of policy as well.

The cumulative deficit is an exponential growth function. The greater the deficit becomes, the greater the interest on it. By financing some of this interest, i.e., plowing some of the interest on the deficit back into the deficit, we have created (more exactly, we have allowed our government to create) an exponential growth function of the cumulative deficit.

All exponential growth functions have an f value which can be assigned to them. So, how do we change the value for f that we (i.e., the U.S. government) are operating at? The federal government is not consciously working a certain value for f. However, there is a certain value for f that is working on it (on all of us) whether we acknowledge it or not. Wherever the federal government is (we are) on f the curve, we can see that we can benefit by being at a value for f which is beyond the peak of the curve. At a certain value beyond the peak, where the TWR goes below 1, we can reap a tremendous benefit, because at that value we have a guarantee that the growth function will be broken. That is, at the value for f where the TWR becomes less than 1, we know we would with certainty go broke if we were gamblers using such an f value.

So, if no one is conscious of what value for f we are using, and given that whatever value for f is being used, de facto, we can benefit by moving the f value closer to 1 (if we are, in fact, beyond the peak of the curve). How can this be accomplished?

We have been focusing on A, the total government revenues. That is, we have focused on increasing revenues (or decreasing spending). However, there has been little, if any, focus on the variance in those revenues. If, according to Mr. Hauser (and I believe he is correct), revenues are directly tied to GDP (more so than tax code policy), then there is something very strong to be said in terms of the variance in GDP.

Ultimately, what we must reduce is G, the growth multiple, per period, in HPRs of the federal deficit. Per the Pythagorean theorem vis-a-vis the formula for estimating the geometric mean, this can be accomplished not only by increasing A, average revenues (or average GDP), but can be equally accomplished by increasing S, the standard deviation or variance in revenues (or the standard deviation or variance in GDP, according to the figures supplied by Hauser's column)! Thus, increasing the variance in GDP reduces the growth rate of the federal deficit by an amount *in excess* of an equivalent increase in the arithmetic average GDP!

As the variable f goes from 0 to 1, the standard deviation and arithmetic average HPRs change. At an f of 0, the standard deviation (or its square, variance) equals 0. As the variance increases, the value for f approaches 1. Thus, by increasing the variance in GDP, we push the f value working on us further to the right of the f curve. However, neither the curve nor its peak changes. The only change is where we are on the curve. Thus, the more we can increase the variance in GDP, the better in terms of dampening the growth of the cumulative federal deficit.

However, our policy has been diametrically opposed to this notion. In times of economic downturn, we have sought stimulus through lower rates and government-subsidized stimulus. In times of expansion, the focus has tended to be on fighting inflation, and a general rise in rates. These policies only help to increase the growth rate of the federal deficit. The mathematics of the situation suggest that the government should not seek to dampen the quarter-to-quarter or year-to-year fluctuations in GDP. We are paying a steep, albeit a hidden, price in terms of a higher growth rate than necessary in the cumulative deficit, by having government and federal policy oriented towards dampening the economic cycles. This is exactly what we should not be doing if we want to minimize the growth rate of the federal deficit.

ADDENDUM TWO

The Misleading Nature of Accrual of Management Fees and Time-Weightings

Oftentimes, when accounts are managed by other persons (managers), the fees charged to the account by the manager are charged on a basis other than monthly (typically, this other basis is to charge fees quarterly). Regulatory agencies (in the United States, for instance) insist that these fees be shown as having been charged monthly. When the fees are actually paid quarterly, the performance tables for such managers must be doctored up by an accounting exercise called *accruing* the fees.

A simplistic example will help demonstrate the misleading nature of fee accrual. Assume a hypothetical $10,000 account, traded by a hypothetical manager over a hypothetical three-month period. Further assume that the only fee the manager charges is a 20% incentive fee. That is, only 20% of the new high equity the manager makes is subject to fees, and for every quarter that ends when the equity is at a new high point, 20% of the difference between the new high equity point and the old high equity point is taken by the manager as the incentive fee. This is not atypical at all of a managed futures account.

Month	Starting Value	Change for Month	Fees Actually Paid	Ending Value	Percent Return
Jan	$10,000			$10,000	0.00%
Feb	$10,000	$20,000		$30,000	200.00%
Mar	$30,000	($15,000)	$1,000	$14,000	−53.33%

The account starts with $10,000, and ends the quarter with $14,000, after paying $1,000 in fees at the end of March. This is consistent with the TWR, which we get by adding 1 to the Percent Return column, and multiplying them together:

$$1 * 3 * .4667 = 1.4$$

However, when we accrue the fees monthly in this example, we get the following:

Month	Starting Value	Change for Month	Accrual of Fees	Ending Value	Percent Return
Jan	$10,000			$10,000	0.00%
Feb	$10,000	$20,000	$4,000	$26,000	160.00%
Mar	$30,000	($15,000)	($3,000)	$18,000	−40.00%

Notice that the net of the fees paid, at the end of the quarter, is still $1,000. However, when we figure the TWR, based on converting the percentage returns to HPRs by adding 1 to them, we get $1 * 2.6 * .6 = 1.56$, which suggests that the account value should have finished the quarter at $15,600.

The discrepancy arises because the nature of accruing fees will cause a reduction in the standard deviation in monthly returns, without a compensating reduction in the arithmetic average monthly return. Thus, it reduces the base of the right-angle triangle without reducing the hypotenuse. The only way the vertical leg (the geometric mean return) can comply is by increasing.

Arguably, one looks at the ending balance in both tables, $14,000, and divides it by the starting balance in both tables, $10,000, and arrives at the same conclusion—that a 40% return was earned. After all, who is going to convert the monthly percentage returns to HPRs, and multiply them together to get a TWR, then subtract 1 from the product to obtain the geometric mean return?

But, this is exactly what is happening! One common performance measure is called VAMI. It represents the value of $1,000 invested at the beginning of the program. In effect, VAMI is simply the TWR at any given month, multiplied by 1,000. For the nonaccrual-based table:

Month	Starting Value	Change for Month	Fees Actually Paid	Ending Value	Percent Return	VAMI
Jan	$10,000			$10,000	0.00%	1000
Feb	$10,000	$20,000		$30,000	200.00%	3000
Mar	$30,000	($15,000)	$1,000	$14,000	−53.33%	1400

With VAMI appended to the table of accrual-based fees:

Month	Starting Value	Change for Month	Accrual of Fees	Ending Value	Percent Return	VAMI
Jan	$10,000			$10,000	0.00%	1000
Feb	$10,000	$20,000	$4,000	$26,000	160.00%	2600
Mar	$30,000	($15,000)	($3,000)	$18,000	−40.00%	1560

This VAMI number *is* looked at, not only by many potential investors as a way to distill all of the accounting nonsense in the performance tables down to a meaningful statistic, it is also heavily relied upon by many services which track account managers. Thus, this misleading nature is leaching throughout the universe of potential investors in many different ways.

Thus, accrual-based accounting of fees is misleading to potential investors because it tends to overstate performance. This example, although extreme, is not atypical and shows a 56% return for the quarter when fees are calculated on an accrual basis, when in fact only a 40% return was earned. Thus, regulatory bodies requiring fee accrual in performance tables are promoting a practice which is misleading, thus doing a disservice to potential investors. Ironically, this is exactly the opposite of what the regulatory bodies should seek to do.

Time-weighting of additions and withdrawals is another misleading notion, widely practiced in the managed money industry. However, this notion tends to diminish what the actual returns were, thus working against the money manager. Typically, time-weighting requires that the returns be computed as a function of how many days the money was available during the period (typically a month). Thus, if someone opens an account on the sixteenth day of a thirty-day month, the money was available to the manager for .5 of the month. The returns for that account for that month would then be multiplied by 2. Thus, if a 10% return was made in that account for that month, the return would be shown as a 20% return. Likewise, a 10% loss for that month would be shown as a 20% loss. To assume a straight-line extrapolation is fictitious enough, but a straight-line extrapolation should be figured in a multiplicative, not an additive, sense. In other words, the 10% gain in this example, if it were to be extrapolated out for the remainder of the month, should be $1.1 * 1.1 = 1.21$, or a 21% gain. Likewise, a 10% loss in this case should be figured as $.9 * .9 = .81$, or a 19% loss for the month.

When the funds are only available for one or a few days of the month, the returns reported become increasingly fallacious. An advisor required to use time-weighting of additions and withdrawals may, in such a case of having an account open one day, losing over 3⅓% on that day, be required to report a loss for that account for the month which exceeds 100%! (The multiplicative method shown here is fallacious, too, only to a lesser extent—you will not get returns exceeding 100%, and it isn't always biased against the manager. However, it, too, is an extrapolation which assumes that the returns for the other segments in the month were without variance to the returns for the segment during which the funds were available.)

These misguided requirements, the accrual of management fees, and time-weightings of additions and withdrawals in returns calculations create an enormous element of fiction. They mislead the public. It is akin to accepting the idea that $2 + 2 = 5$, just because some grumbling little bug says it does. Investment managers and the investment public would all be better off in a world where the regulatory bodies didn't insist on such misleading mathematical concoctions.

REFERENCES

1. Thomas S. Kuhn, *The Structure of Scientific Revolution,* The University of Chicago Press, 1962.
2. John von Neumann and Osker Morgenstern, *Theory of Games and Economic Behavior,* Princeton University Press, 1944.
3. C. E. Shannon, "A Mathematical Theory of Communication," *Bell System Technical Journal,* Oct. 1948, pp. 379–656.
4. J. L. Kelly, Jr., "A New Interpretation of Information Rate," *Bell System Technical Journal,* July 1956, pp. 917–926.
5. Edward O. Thorp, *Beat the Dealer,* New York: Vintage Books, Random House, Inc., 1966.
6. E. O. Thorp, "The Kelly Money Management System," *Gambling Times,* Dec. 1980, pp. 91–92.
7. Fred Gehm, *Commodity Market Money Management,* Wiley, 1983.
8. Ralph Vince, *Portfolio Management Formulas,* Wiley, 1990.
9. Ralph Vince, *The Mathematics of Money Management,* New York: Wiley, 1992.

2
Laws of Growth, Utility, and Finite Streams

Since this book deals with the mathematics involving growth, we must discuss the laws of growth. When dealing with growth in mathematical terms, we can discuss it in terms of growth functions or of the corresponding growth rates.

We can speak of growth functions as falling into three distinct categories, where each category is associated with a growth *rate*. Figure 2.1 portrays these three categories as lines B, C, and D, and their growth rates as A, B, and C, respectively. Each growth function has its growth rate immediately to its left.

Thus, for growth function B, the linear growth function, its growth rate is line A. Further, although B is a growth function itself, it also represents the growth rate for function C, the exponential growth rate.

Notice that there are three growth functions, *linear, exponential,* and *hyperbolic.* Thus, the hyperbolic growth function has an exponential growth rate, the exponential growth function has a linear growth rate, and the linear growth function has a flat-line growth rate.

The x and y axes are important here. If we are discussing growth functions (B, C, or D), the Y axis represents quantity and the X axis represents time. If we are discussing growth rates, the y axis represents quantity change with respect to time, and the x axis represents quantity.

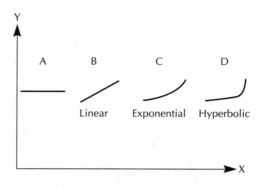

FIGURE 2.1

When we speak of growth rates and functions in general, we often speak of the growth of a population of something. The first of the three major growth functions is the linear growth function, line B, and its rate, line A. Members of a population characterized by linear growth tend to easily find a level of coexistence.

Next, we have the exponential growth function, line C, and its growth rate, which is linear, line B. Here, we find competition among the members of the population, and a survival-of-the-fittest principle setting in. In the exponential growth function, however, it is possible for a mutation to appear, which has a selective advantage, and establish itself.

Finally, in the hyperbolic growth function, line D, and its (exponential) growth rate, line C, we find a different story. Unlike the exponential growth function, which has a linear growth rate, this one's growth rate is itself exponential. That is, the greater the quantity, the faster the growth rate! Thus, the hyperbolic function, unlike the exponential function, reaches a point that we call a *singularity*. That is, it reaches a point where it becomes infinitely large, a vertical asymptote. This is not true of the exponential growth function, which simply becomes larger and larger. In the hyperbolic function, we also find competition among the members of the population, and a survival-of-the-fittest characteristic. However, at a certain point in the evolution of a hyperbolic function, it becomes nearly impossible for a mutation with a selective advantage to establish itself, since the rest of the population is growing at such a rapid rate.

In either the exponential or hyperbolic growth functions, if there are functional links between the competing species within the population, it can cause any of the following:

1. Increased competition among the partners; or
2. Mutual stabilization among the partners; or
3. Extinction of all members of the population.

The notion of populations is also a recurring theme throughout this book, and it is nearly impossible to discuss the mathematics of growth without discussing populations. The mathematics of growth is the corpus callosum between population growth and the new framework presented in this book.

HUMAN POPULATION GROWTH

After about the first two million years of our evolution, there were at most ten million humans on the earth. Then, around ten thousand years ago, with the New Stone Age, the human population began to increase at a faster rate. Although many of the figures are sketchy, we can approximate the human population of the earth for the last two thousand years (Figure 2.2):

Year	Approx. Pop. in Billions
0	.25
1650	.5
1850	1
1930	2
1990	5.3

If we do some simple mathematical extrapolation, we can quickly see that the growth function that fits these points is hyperbolic with the singularity, the asymptote where the population shoots up to infinity, around the middle of the next century!

The reason the function is hyperbolic is that life expectancy keeps increasing. More females are reaching childbearing age. This results in an increase in the time it takes for the population to double, which is already less than the expected life span!

Bear in mind that this chart, these population numbers we have reached, are after such catastrophes as the black death of the fourteenth century, which wiped out about two-thirds of Europe, a couple of world wars (the most recent of which wiped out about fifty million of which

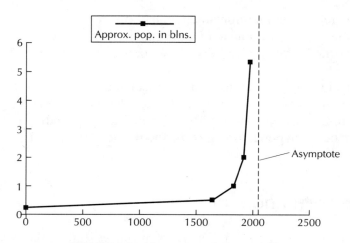

FIGURE 2.2   Human population growth.

twenty-seven million were in Russia alone!), along with everything else nature has challenged us with along the way. Thus, even something catastrophic enough to wipe out two-thirds of Europe today would only have the effect of pushing the asymptote a little further out in time.

Projections for future population vary, with probably the most optimistic being that of an eight to nine billion world population figure by 2075. This is predicated upon birth and death rates leveling off on all continents. A 1990 report by the UN is not quite so optimistic, calling for world population to reach 11.3 billion by the end of the next century if there is some form of worldwide population control; otherwise, the figure could easily top fourteen billion.

The problem, as is so visually apparent in Figure 2.2, is that population growth is a hyperbolic function with an asymptote somewhere around the middle of the next century. These are very near the historical facts and their mathematical extrapolation into the future.

Since it is physically impossible for us to become infinite in population, what can we expect? From looking at the chart in Figure 2.2, you can see that population size is going to be a major problem, at present rates, well before the middle of the next century.

There are a number of catastrophic scenarios that can easily come to mind. They pretty much fall into two broad scenarios, the first of which is man vs. man—some type of World War III scenario. There is, undoubtedly, ample evidence to assume this is a distinct possibility that may thin out our ranks.

There is the broad nature-versus-man scenario, especially if the man-versus-man scenario does not manifest soon, which we may be witnessing via the many burgeoning viruses and resilient bacteria about the world. Not only the AIDS virus, but there are also other more contagious, but equally deadly, *airborne* or otherwise highly contagious viruses by which we are now being assaulted, such as Ebola or the human parvovirus, which threaten to annihilate us entirely.

There is an odd, but perhaps quite likely scenario with a semioptimistic tone. I call this the space station scenario, wherein we begin, in the next century, to populate outside of this planet, thus insuring our survival as a species. This scenario can, long term, accommodate a much greater population than can the earth alone. This scenario, however, doesn't mean that overpopulation on the earth would be alleviated; it simply allows for a larger human population in all.

Clearly, as we paint scenarios, there is an overriding theme. We must somehow embrace a worldwide population control policy or we will have one bestowed upon us by natural course. Only a highly controlled population size, with a *linear* growth function (such as the policy imposed in The People's Republic of China) pressing ever so gently on the resources of the earth, can insure our long-term peaceful existence.

Anything to the contrary is simple mathematical ignorance of hyperbolic growth functions! This is exemplified in the extreme by the so-called green movement. I am not faulting the principles of this movement. Ultimately, the so-called green principles are necessary. They are, however, secondary to the problem we have of a population which grows hyperbolically by its very nature. As this continues, we will realize environmental disaster, whether from the excessive methane caused if we all ride horses, thus depleting the ozone layer, or if we all drive electric carts with the concomitant environmental problems such electric requirements carry.

A motorist caught in a traffic jam may attribute it to the inefficiency of modern technological life, but the traffic jam he is the prisoner of is the result of population growth and it would be there regardless of whether he and the other motorists were in modern automobiles or horse-drawn carriages.

The fact that we have a population which grows hyperbolically by its very nature is the single biggest challenge to us, and it would be silly to discuss growth rates at this point in history, in any context, without discussing them in the context of population growth.

Enough on that. Back to growth in general, and trading in particular.

Trading is exponential, *not* hyperbolic. However, if you had someone who would give you money to trade if your performance came in as promised, and that person had virtually unlimited funds, then your trading would be hyperbolic. This sounds like managed money. The problem faced by money managers is the caveat laid on the money manager by the individual of unlimited wealth: *if your performance comes in as promised.* In the last chapter in this book, we will discuss techniques to address this caveat.

MAXIMIZING EXPECTED AVERAGE COMPOUND GROWTH

Thus far, in this book, as well as in its two predecessors, we have looked at finding a value for f which was asymptotically dominant. That is, we have sought a single value for f for a given market system, which, if there truly was independence between the trades, would maximize geometric growth with certainty as the number of trades (or holding periods) approached infinity. That is, we would end up with greater wealth in the very long run with a probability that approached certainty, than we would using any other money management strategy.

Recall, that if we have only one play, we maximize growth by maximizing the arithmetic average holding period return (i.e., $f = 1$). If we have an infinite number of plays, we maximize growth by maximizing the geometric average holding period return (i.e., f = optimal f). However, *the f which is truly optimal is a function of the length of time—the number of finite holding period returns—that we are going to play.*

For one holding period return, the optimal f will always be 1.0 for a positive arithmetic mathematical expectation game. If we bet at any value for f other than 1.0, and quit after only one holding period, we will not have maximized our expected average geometric growth. What we regard as the optimal f will only be optimal if you were to play for an infinite number of holding periods. The f that is truly optimal starts at one for a positive arithmetic mathematical expectation game, and converges towards what we call the optimal f as the number of holding periods approaches infinity.

To see this, consider again our two-to-one coin toss game where we have determined the optimal f to be .25. That is, if the coin tosses are independent of previous tosses, by betting 25% of our stake on each and every play, we will maximize our geometric growth with certainty as the length of this game, the number of tosses (i.e., the number of holding periods) approaches infinity. That is, our expected average geometric growth—what we would expect to end up with, as an expected value, given every possible combination of outcomes—would be greatest if we bet 25% per play.

Consider the first toss. There is a 50% probability of winning two dollars, and a 50% probability of losing two dollars. At the second toss, there is a 25% chance of winning two dollars on the first toss and winning two dollars on the second, a 25% chance of winning two dollars on the first and losing one dollar on the second, a 25% chance of losing one dollar on the first and winning two dollars on the second, and a 25% chance of losing one dollar on the first and losing one dollar on the second (we know these probabilities to be true because we have already stated the prerequisite that these events are independent—see "Stochastic Independence" in the next chapter). The combinations bloom out in time in a tree-like fashion. Since we had only two scenarios (heads and tails) in this scenario spectrum, there are only two branches off of each node in the tree. If we had more scenarios in this spectrum, there would be that many more branches off of each node in this tree:

	Toss #	
{1}	{2}	{3}
		heads
	heads	
		tails
heads		
		heads
	tails	
		tails
		heads
	heads	
		tails
tails		
		heads
	tails	
		tails

If we bet 25% of our stake on the first toss and quit, we will not have maximized our expected average compound growth (EACG).

What if we quit after the second toss? What, then, should we optimally bet, knowing that we maximize our expected average compound gain by betting at $f = 1$ when we are going to quit after one play, and betting at the optimal f if we are going to play for an infinite length of time?

If we go back and optimize f, allowing there to be a different f value used for the first play as well as the second play, with the intent of maximizing what our average geometric mean HPR would be at the end of the second play, we would find the following. First, the optimal f for quitting after two plays in this game approaches the asymptotic optimal, going from 1.0 if we quit after one play to .5 for both the first play and the second. That is, if we were to quit after the second play, we should optimally bet .5 on both the first and second plays to maximize growth. (Remember, we allowed for the first play to be an f value different from the second, yet they both came out the same: .5 in this case. It is a fact that if you are looking to maximize growth, the f that is optimal—for finite as well as infinite streams—is uniform.)

We can see this if we take the first two possible combinations of tosses:

Toss #	
{1}	{2}
	heads
heads	
	tails
	heads
tails	
	tails

Which can be represented by the following outcomes:

Toss #	
{1}	{2}
	2
2	
	−1
	2
−1	
	−1

These outcomes can be expressed as holding period returns for various f values. In the following, it is shown for an f of .5 for the first toss, as well as for an f of .5 for the second:

	Toss #
{1}	{2}
	2
2	
	.5
	2
.5	
	.5

Now, we can express all tosses subsequent to the first toss as TWRs by multiplying by the subsequent tosses on the tree. The numbers following the last toss on the tree (the numbers in parentheses) are the last TWRs taken to the root of $1/n$, where n equals the number of HPRs, or tosses—in this case two—and represents the geometric mean HPR for that terminal node on the tree:

	Toss #
{1}	{2}
	4 (2.0)
2	
	1 (1.0)
	1 (1.0)
.5	
	.25 (.5)

Now, if we total up the geometric mean HPRs and take their arithmetic average, we obtain the *expected average compound return*, in this case:

$$
\begin{array}{c}
2.0 \\
1.0 \\
1.0 \\
\underline{.5} \\
\dfrac{4.5}{4} = 1.125
\end{array}
$$

Thus, if we were to quit after two plays, and yet do this same thing over an infinite number of times (i.e., quit after two plays), we would optimally bet .5 of our stake on each and every play, thus maximizing our EACG.

Notice that we did not bet with an f of 1.0 on the first play, even though that is what would have maximized our expected average compound growth if we had quit at one play. Instead, if we are planning on quitting after two plays, we maximize our EACG growth by betting at .5 both on the first play and the second play.

Notice that the f that is optimal in order to maximize growth is uniform for all plays, yet it is a function of how long you will play. If you are to quit after only one play, the f that is optimal is the f that maximizes the arithmetic mean HPR (which is always an f of 1.0 for a positive expectation game, 0.0 for a negative expectation game). If you are playing a positive expectation game, the f that is optimal continues to decrease as the length of time after which you quit grows, and, asymptotically, if you play for an infinitely long time, the f that is optimal is that which maximizes the geometric mean HPR. In a negative expectation game, the f which is optimal simply stays at zero.

However, the f that you use to maximize growth is always uniform, and, that uniform amount is a function of where you intend to quit the game. If you are playing the two-to-one coin toss game, and you intend to quit after one play, you have an f value that provides for optimal growth of 1.0. If you intend to quit after two plays, you have an f that is optimal for maximizing growth of .5 on the first toss, and .5 on the second. Notice, you do not bet 1.0 on the first toss if you are planning on maximizing the EACG by quitting at the end of the second play. Likewise, if you are planning on playing for an infinitely long period of time, you would optimally bet .25 on the first toss and .25 on each subsequent toss.

Note the key word there is *infinitely,* not *indefinitely.* All streams are finite—we are all going to die eventually. Therefore, when we speak of the optimal f as the f that maximizes expected average compound return, we are speaking of that value which maximizes it if played for an infinitely long period of time. Actually, it is slightly suboptimal because none of us will be able to play for an infinitely long time. And, the f that will maximize EACG will be slightly above—will have us take slightly heavier positions—than what we are calling the optimal f.

What if we were to quit after three tosses? Shouldn't the f which then maximizes expected average compound growth be lower still than the .5 it is when quitting after two plays, yet still be greater than the .25 optimal for an infinitely long game?

Let's examine the tree of combinations here

	Toss #	
{1}	{2}	{3}
		heads
	heads	
		tails
heads		
		heads
	tails	
		tails
		heads
	heads	
		tails
tails		
		heads
	tails	
		tails

Converting these to outcomes yields:

	Toss #	
{1}	{2}	{3}
		2
	2	
		−1
2		
		2
	−1	
		−1
		2
	2	
		−1
−1		
		2
	−1	
		−1

If we go back with a computer and iterate to that value for f which maximizes expected average compound growth when quitting after three tosses, we find it to be .37868. Therefore, converting the outcomes to HPRs based upon a .37868 value for f at each toss yields:

	Toss #	
{1}	{2}	{3}
		1.757369
	1.757369	
		.621316
1.757369		
		1.757369
	.621316	
		.621316
		1.757369
	1.757369	
		.621316
.621316		
		1.757369
	.621316	
		.621316

Now we can express all tosses subsequent to the first toss as TWRs by multiplying by the subsequent tosses on the tree. The numbers following the last toss on the tree (the numbers in parentheses) are the last TWRs taken to the root of $1/n$, where n equals the number of HPRs, or tosses, in this case three, and represent the geometric mean HPR for that terminal node on the tree:

		Toss #	
{1}	{2}	{3}	
		5.427324	(1.757365)
	3.088329		
		1.918831	(1.242641)
1.757369			
		1.918848	(1.242644)
	1.09188		
		.678409	(.87868)
		1.918824	(1.242639)
	1.091875		
		.678401	(.878676)

Toss # (*Continued*)

{1}	{2}	{3}	
.621316			
		.678406	(.878678)
	.386036		
		.239851	(.621318)

$$\frac{8.742641}{8} = 1.09283 \text{ is the expected average compound growth (EACG)}$$

If you are the slightest bit skeptical of this, I suggest you go back over the last few examples, either with pen and pencil or computer, and find a value for f which results in a greater EACG than the values presented. Allow yourself the liberty of a nonuniform f—that is, an f that is allowed to change at each play. You'll find that you get the same answers as we have, and that f is uniform, although a function of the length of the game. From this, we can summarize the following conclusions:

1. To maximize the expected average compound growth (EACG), we always end up with a uniform f. That is, the value for f is uniform from one play to the next.

2. The f that is optimal in terms of maximizing the EACG is a function of the length of the game. For positive expectation games, it starts at 1.0, the value that maximizes the arithmetic mean HPR, diminishes slightly each play, and asymptotically approaches that value which maximizes the geometric mean HPR (which we have been calling—and will call throughout the sequel—the optimal f).

3. Since all streams are finite in length, regardless of how long, we will always be ever-so-slightly suboptimal by trading at what we call the optimal f, regardless of how long we trade. Yet, the difference diminishes with each holding period. Ultimately, we are to the left of the peak of what was truly optimal. This is not to say that everything mentioned about the $n + 1$ dimensional landscape of leverage space—the penalties and payoffs of where you are with respect to the optimal f for each market system—aren't true. It is true, however, that the landscape is a function of the number of holding periods at which you quit. The landscape we project with the techniques in this book are the asymptotic altitudes—what the landscape approaches as we continue to play.

To see this, let's continue with our two-to-one coin toss. In the graph (Figure 2.3), we can see the value for f, which optimally maximizes our expected average compound growth for quitting at one play through eight plays. Notice how it approaches the optimal f of .25, the value which maximizes growth asymptotically, as the number of holding periods approaches infinity.

Two-to-One Coin Toss Game

Quitting after HPR #	f which maximizes EACG
1	1.0
2	.5
3	.37868
4	.33626
5	.3148
6	.3019
7	.2932
8	.2871
.	.
.	.
.	.
infinity	.25 (this is the value we refer to as the optimal f)

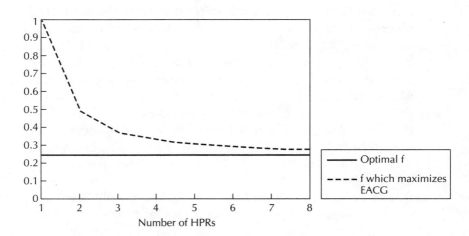

FIGURE 2.3 Optimal f as an asymptote.

In reality, if we trade with what we are calling in this text the optimal f, we will always be slightly suboptimal, the degree of which diminishes as more and more holding periods elapse. If we knew exactly how many holding periods we were going to trade for, we could then use that value for f which maximizes EACG (which would be slightly greater than the optimal f) and be truly optimal. Unfortunately, we rarely know exactly how many holding periods we are going to play for, and there is consolation in the fact that what we are calling the optimal f approaches what would be optimal to maximize EACG as more holding periods elapse. In the final chapter of this book, we will see the *continuous dominance* techniques, which allow us to approximate the notion of maximizing EACG when there is an active/inactive equity split (i.e., anytime someone is trading less aggressively than optimal f).

Note that none of these notions is addressed or even alluded to in the older mean-variance, risk-return models. The older models disregard leverage and it's workings almost entirely. This is one more reason to opt for this new model.

UTILITY THEORY

The discussion of utility theory is brought up in this book since, oftentimes, geometric mean maximizers are criticized for being able to maximize only the ln x case of utility; that is, they seek to maximize only wealth, not investor satisfaction. This book attempts to show that geometric mean maximization can be applicable, regardless of one's utility preference function. Therefore, we must, at this point, discuss utility theory, in general, as a foundation.

Utility theory is often attacked as being an ivory-tower, academic construct to explain investor behavior. Unfortunately, most of these attacks come from people who have made the a priori assumption that all investor utility functions are ln x; that is, they seek to maximize wealth. While this author is not a great proponent of utility theory, I accept it for lack of a better explanation for investor preferences. However, I strongly feel that if an investor's utility function is other than ln x, the markets, and investing in general, are poor places to deal with this or to try to maximize one's utility—you're on the n + 1 dimensional landscape discussed in Chapter 1 regardless of your utility preference curve, and you will pay the consequences in real currency for being suboptimal. In short, the markets are a bad place to find out you are not a wealth maximizer. The psychiatrist's couch may be a more gentle environment in which to deal with that.

THE EXPECTED UTILITY THEOREM

A guy in an airport has $500, but needs $600 for a ticket he *must* have. He is offered a bet with a 50% probability of winning $100, and a 50% probability of losing $500. Is this a good bet? In this instance, where we assume it to be a life-and-death situation where he must have the ticket, it *is* a good bet.

The mathematical expectation of utility is vastly different in this instance than the mathematical expectation of wealth. Since, if we subscribe to utility theory, we determine *good bets* based on their mathematical expectation of *utility* rather than *wealth,* we assume that the mathematical expectation of utility in this instance is positive, even though wealth is not. Think of the words *utility* and *satisfaction* as meaning the same thing in this discussion.

Thus, we have what is called the *expected utility theorem,* which states that *investors posses a utility of wealth function,* U(x), *where x is wealth, that they will seek to maximize. Thus, investors will opt for those investment decisions that maximize their utility of wealth function.* Only when the utility preference function $U(x) = \ln x,$ that is, when the utility, or satisfaction, of wealth, equals the wealth, will the expected utility theorem yield the same selection as wealth maximization.

CHARACTERISTICS OF UTILITY PREFERENCE FUNCTIONS

There are five main characteristics of utility preference functions:

1. Utility functions are unique up to a positive linear transformation. Thus, a utility preference function, such as the preceding one, $\ln x,$ will lead to the same investments being selected as a utility function of $25 + \ln x,$ as it would be a utility function of $7 * \ln x$ or one of the form $(\ln x)/1.453456.$ That is, a utility function which is affected by a positive constant (added, subtracted, multiplied, or divided) will result in the same investments being selected. Thus, it will lead to the same set of investments maximizing utility as before the positive constant affects the function.

2. More is preferred to less. In economic literature, this is often referred to as *nonsatiation*. In other words, a utility function must never result in a choice for less wealth over more wealth when the outcomes are certain or their probabilities equal. Since utility must, therefore, increase as wealth increases, the first derivative of utility, with respect to wealth, must be positive. That is:

$$U'(x) >= 0 \qquad [2.01]$$

Given utility as the vertical axis and wealth as the horizontal axis, then the utility preference curve must never have a negative slope.

The ln x case of utility preference functions shows a first derivative of x^{-1}.

3. There are three possible assumptions regarding an investor's feelings towards risk, also called his *risk aversion*. He is either averse to, neutral to, or seeks risk. These can all be defined in terms of a fair gamble. If we assume a fair game, such as coin tossing, winning one dollar on heads and losing one dollar on tails, we can see that the arithmetic expectation of wealth is zero. A risk-averse individual would not accept this bet; whereas, a risk seeker would accept it. The investor who is risk-neutral would be indifferent to accepting this bet.

Risk aversion pertains to the second derivative of the utility preference function, or $U''(x)$. A risk-averse individual will show a negative second derivative, a risk seeker a positive second derivative, and one who is risk-neutral will show a zero second derivative of the utility preference function.

Figure 2.4 depicts the three basic types of utility preference functions, based on $U''(x)$, the investor's level of risk aversion. The ln x case of utility preference functions shows neutral risk aversion. The investor is indifferent to a fair gamble.* The ln x case of utility preference functions shows a second derivative of $-x^{-2}$.

4. The fourth characteristic of utility preference functions pertains to how an investor's levels of risk aversion change with changes in wealth.

---

* Actually, investors should reject a fair gamble. Since the amount of money an investor has to work with is finite, there is a lower absorbing barrier. It can be shown that if an investor accepts fair gambles repeatedly, it is simply a matter of time before the lower absorbing barrier is met. That is, if you keep on accepting fair gambles, eventually you will go broke with a probability approaching certainty.

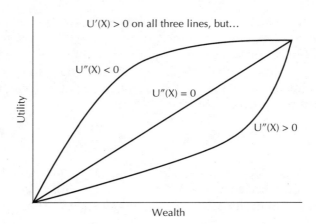

FIGURE 2.4   Three basic types of utility functions.

This is referred to as *absolute risk aversion*. Again, there are three possible categories. First is the individual who exhibits increasing absolute risk aversion. As wealth increases, he holds fewer dollars in risky assets. Next is the individual with constant absolute risk aversion. As his wealth increases, he holds the same dollar amount in risk assets. Last is the individual who displays decreasing absolute risk aversion. As this individual's wealth increases, he is willing to hold more dollars in risky assets.

The mathematical formulation for defining absolute risk aversion, $A(x)$ is as follows:

$$A(x) = \frac{-U''(x)}{U'(x)} \qquad\qquad [2.02]$$

Now, if we want to see how absolute risk aversion changes with a change in wealth, we would take the first derivative of $A(x)$ with respect to x (wealth), obtaining $A'(x)$. Thus, an individual with increasing absolute risk aversion would have $A'(x) > 0$, constant absolute risk aversion would see $A'(x) = 0$, and decreasing absolute risk aversion has $A'(x) < 0$.

The ln x case of utility preference functions shows *decreasing* absolute risk aversion. For the ln x case

$$A(x) = \frac{-(-x^{-2})}{x^{-1}} = x^{-1} \qquad \text{and} \qquad A'(x) = -x^{-2} < 0$$

5. The fifth characteristic of utility preference functions pertains to how the percentage of wealth invested in risky assets changes with changes in wealth. This is referred to as *relative risk aversion*. That is, this pertains to how your percentages in risky assets change, rather than how your dollar amounts change, with respect to changes in wealth. Again, there are three possible categories: increasing, constant, and decreasing relative risk aversion, where the percentages invested in risky assets increase, stay the same, or decline, respectively.

The mathematical formulation for defining relative risk aversion, $R(x)$ is as follows:

$$R(x) = \frac{(-x * U''(x))}{U'(x)} = x * A(x) \qquad [2.03]$$

Therefore, $R'(x)$, the first derivative of relative risk aversion, indicates how relative risk aversion changes with respect to changes in wealth. So, individuals who show increasing, constant, or decreasing relative risk aversion will then show positive, zero, and negative $R'(x)$, respectively.

The $\ln x$ case of utility preference functions shows *constant* relative risk aversion. For the $\ln x$ case

$$R(x) = \frac{(-x*(-x^{-2}))}{x^{-1}} = 1 \qquad \text{and} \qquad R'(x) = 0$$

ALTERNATE ARGUMENTS TO CLASSICAL UTILITY THEORY

Readers should be aware that utility theory, although broadly accepted, is not universally accepted as an explanation of investor behavior. For example, R. C. Wentworth contends, with reference to the expected utility theorem, that the use of the mean is an ad hoc, unjustified assumption. His theory is that players assume that the mode, rather than the mean, will prevail, and will act to maximize this.

I personally find Wentworth's work in this area particularly interesting.* There are some rather interesting aspects to these papers. First,

---

* See "Utility, Survival, and Time: Decision Strategies Under Favorable Uncertainty," and "A Theory of Risk Management Under Favorable Uncertainty," both by R. C. Wentworth, unpublished. 8072 Broadway Terrace, Oakland, CA 94611.

classical utility theory is directly attacked, which automatically alienates every professor in every management science department in the world. The theoretical foundation paradigm of the nonlinear *utility-of-wealth* function is sacred to these people. Wentworth draws parallels between *mode maximizers* and evolution; hence, Wentworth calls his the *survival hypothesis*. A thumbnail sketch of the comparison with classical utility theory would appear as:

Utility Theory

'One-shot', risky decision making	+	Nonlinear utility-of-wealth function	==>	Observed behavior

Survival Hypothesis

'One-shot', risky decision making	+	Expansion into equivalent time series	==>	Identical observed behavior

Furthermore, there are some interesting experiments in biology which tend to support Wentworth's ideas, which ask the question why, for instance, should bumblebees search for nectar, in a controlled experiment, according to the dictates of classical utility theory?

So, why mention classical utility theory at all? It is not the purpose of this book to presuppose anything regarding utility theory. However, there is an interrelationship between utility and this new framework in asset allocation, and if one does subscribe to a utility framework notion, then they will be shown how this applies. This portion of the book is directed towards those readers unfamiliar with the notion of utility preference curves. However, it does not take a position on the validity of utility functions, and the reader should be made aware that there are other non-utility-based criteria which may explain investor behavior.

FINDING YOUR UTILITY PREFERENCE CURVE

Whether one subscribes to classical utility theory, considering that it is better to know yourself than not know yourself, we will now detail a technique for determining your own utility preference function. What follows is an adaptation from *The Commodity Futures Game, Who Wins? Who Loses? Why?* by Tewles, Harlow, and Stone.[1]

To begin with, you should determine two extreme values, one positive and the other negative, which should represent extreme trade outcomes. Typically, you should make this value be three to five times greater than the largest amounts you would typically expect to win or lose on the next trade.

Let's suppose you expect, in the best case, to win $5,000 on a trade, and lose $3,000. Thus, we can make our extremes $20,000 on the upside and −$10,000 on the downside.

Next, set up a table as follows, with a leftmost column called *Probabilities of Best Outcome,* and give it ten rows with values progressing from 1.0 to 0 by increments of .1. Your next column should be called *Probabilities of Worst Outcome,* and those probabilities are simply 1 minus the probabilities of the best outcome on that row. The third column will be labeled *Certainty Equivalent.* In the first row, you will put the value of the best outcome, and in the last row, the value of the worst outcome. Thus, your table should look like this:

P (Best Outcome)	P (Worst Outcome)	Certainty Equivalent	Computed Utility
1.0	0	$20,000	
.9	.1		
.8	.2		
.7	.3		
.6	.4		
.5	.5		
.4	.6		
.3	.7		
.2	.8		
.1	.9		
0	1.0	−$10,000	

Now, we introduce the notion of *certainty equivalents.* A certainty equivalent is an amount you would accept in lieu of a trading opportunity or an amount you might pay to sidestep a trade opportunity.

You should now fill in column three, the certainty equivalents. For the first row, the one where we entered $20,000, this simply means you would accept $20,000 in cash right now, rather than take a trade with a

100% probability of winning $20,000. Likewise, with the last row where we have filled in $10,000, this simply means you would be willing to pay $10,000 not to have to take a trade with a 100% chance of losing $10,000.

Now, on the second row, you must determine a certainty equivalent for a trade with a 90% chance of winning $20,000 and a 10% chance of losing $10,000. What would you be willing to accept in cash instead of taking this trade? Remember, this is real money with real buying power, and the rewards or consequences of this transaction will be immediate and in cash. Let's suppose it's worth $15,000 to you. That is, for $15,000 in cash, handed to you right now, you will forego this opportunity of a 90% chance of winning $20,000 and 10% chance of losing $10,000.

You should complete the table for the certainty equivalent columns. For instance, when you are on the second to last row, you are, in effect, asking yourself how much you would be willing to pay not to have to accept a 10% chance of winning $20,000 with a 90% chance of losing $10,000. Since you are willing to pay, you should enter this certainty equivalent as a negative amount.

When you have completed the third column, you must now calculate the fourth column, the *Computed Utility* column. The formula for computed utility is simply:

$$\text{Computed Utility} = U * P \text{ (best outcome)} + V * P \text{ (worst outcome)} \quad [2.04]$$

where U = given constant, equal to 1.0 in this instance
          V = given constant, equal to −1.0 in this instance

Thus, for the second row in the table:

$$\text{Computed utility} = 1 * .9 - 1 * .1$$
$$= .9 - .1$$
$$= .8$$

When you are finished calculating the computed utility columns, your table might look like this:

P (Best Outcome)	P (Worst Outcome)	Certainty Equivalent	Computed Utility
1.0	0	20,000	1.0
.9	.1	15,000	.8
.8	.2	10,000	.6
.7	.3	7,500	.4
.6	.4	5,000	.2
.5	.5	2,500	0
.4	.6	800	−.2
.3	.7	−1,500	−.4
.2	.8	−3,000	−.6
.1	.9	−4,000	−.8
0	1.0	−10,000	−1.0

You then graphically plot the certainty equivalents as the *x* axis, and the computed utilities as the *y* axis. Our completed utility function looks as is shown in Figure 2.5.

Now you should repeat the test, only with different best and worst outcomes. Select a certainty equivalent from the preceding table to act as *best outcome,* and one for *worst outcome* as well. Suppose we choose $10,000 and −$4,000. Notice that the computed utilities associated with

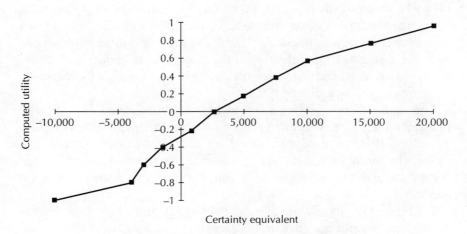

FIGURE 2.5   Example utility function.

certainty equivalents are .6 with $10,000 and −.8 with −$4,000. Thus, *U* and *V*, in determining computed utilities in this next table, will be .6 and −.8, respectively. Again, assign certainty equivalents and calculate the corresponding computed utilities:

P (Best Outcome)	P (Worst Outcome)	Certainty Equivalent	Computed Utility
1.0	0	10,000	.6
.9	.1	8,000	.46
.8	.2	6,000	.32
.7	.3	5,000	.18
.6	.4	4,000	.04
.5	.5	2,500	−.10
.4	.6	500	−.24
.3	.7	−1,000	−.38
.2	.8	−2,000	−.52
.1	.9	−3,000	−.66
0	1.0	−4,000	−.80

And, again, you should plot these values. You should repeat the process a few times, and keep plotting all the values on the same chart. What you will probably begin to see is some scattering to the values; that is, they will not all neatly fit on the same line. The scattering of these values reveals information about yourself, in that the scattering represents inconsistencies in your decisions. Usually, scattering is more pronounced near the extremes (left and right) of the chart. This is normal and simply indicates areas where you have probably not had a lot of experience winning and losing money.

The shape of the curve is also important, and should be looked at with respect to the earlier section entitled *Characteristics of Utility Preference Functions*. It is not at all uncommon for the curve to be imperfect, not simply the textbook concave-up, concave-down, or straight-line shapes. Again, this reveals information about yourself, and warrants careful analysis.

Ultimately, the most conducive form of utility preference function for maximizing wealth is a straight line pointing upwards, decreasing absolute risk aversion, constant relative risk aversion, and near indifference to a fair gamble; i.e., we are indifferent to a gamble with anything less than the very slightest positive arithmetic mathematical expectation. If your line is anything less than this, then this may be the time for you to reflect upon what you want as well as *why,* and perhaps make necessary personal changes.

UTILITY AND THE NEW FRAMEWORK

This book does not take a stand regarding utility theory, other than this: ***Regardless** of your utility preference curve, you are somewhere in the leverage space of Figure 1.2 for individual games, and somewhere in the n + 1 space dimensional leverage space for multiple simultaneous games, and you reap the benefits of this as well as pay the consequences **no matter what your utility preference.***

Oftentimes, the geometric mean criterion is criticized as it only strives to maximize wealth, and it only maximizes utility for the $\ln x$ function.

Actually, if someone does not subscribe to a $\ln x$ utility preference function, they can still maximize utility much as we are maximizing wealth with optimal f, except they will have a different value for optimal f at each holding period. That is, if someone's utility preference function is other than $\ln x$ (wealth maximization), then their optimal f to (asymptotically) maximize utility is uniform, while at the same time, their optimal f to maximize wealth is nonuniform. In other words, if, as you make more money, your utility is such that you are willing to risk less, then your optimal f will decrease as each holding period elapses.

Do not get this confused with the notion, presented earlier, that the f that is optimal for maximizing expected average compound growth is a function of the number of holding periods at which you quit. It still is, but the idea presented here is that the f that is optimal to maximize utility is not uniform throughout the time period. For example, we have seen in our two-to-one coin toss game that if we were planning on quitting after three plays, three holding periods, we would maximize growth by betting .37868 on each and every play. That is, we uniformly bet .37868 for all three plays.

Now, if we're looking to maximize utility, and our utility function were other than that of maximizing wealth, we would not have a uniform f value to bet on each and every play. Rather, we would have a different f value to bet on each and every play.

Thus, it is possible to maximize utility with the given approach (for utility preference functions other than $\ln x$), provided you use a *nonuni-*

form value for *f* from one holding period to the next. When utility preference is ln *x*—that is, when one prefers wealth maximization—the *f* that
is optimal is always uniform. Thus, the optimal *f* is the same from one
play to the next. When utility preference is other than ln *x*, wealth maximization, a nonuniform optimal *f* value from one holding period to the
next is called for.

Like maximizing wealth, utility can also be maximized in the very
same fashion that we are maximizing wealth. This can be accomplished
by assigning *utils*, rather than a dollar value for the outcomes to each
scenario. A util is simply a unit of satisfaction. The scenario set must also
contain negative util scenarios, just as in wealth maximization, you must
have a scenario which encompasses losing money. Also, the (arithmetic)
mathematical expectation of the scenario set must be positive in terms
of utils, or negative if it improves the overall mix of components.

But, how do you determine the nonuniform value for *f* as you go
through holding periods when your utility preference curve is other than
ln *x*? As each new holding period is encountered, and you update the
outcome values (specified in utils) as your account equity itself changes,
you will get a new optimal *f* value, which, divided by the largest losing
scenario (specified in utils), yields an optimal *f*$ value (also specified in
utils), and you will know how many contracts to trade. The process is
simple; you simply substitute utils in lieu of dollars. The only other thing
you need to do is keep track of your account's cumulative utils (i.e., the
surrogate for equity). Notice that, if you do this and your utility preference function is other than ln *x*, you will actually end up with a nonuniform optimal *f*, in terms of *dollars*, from one holding period to the next.

For example, if we are again faced with a coin toss game which offered
us two dollars on heads being tossed, and a loss of one dollar if tails were
tossed, how much should we bet? We know that if we want to maximize
wealth, and we were going to play this game repeatedly, and we had to
play each subsequent play with money that we started the game with, we
should optimally bet 25% of our stake on each and every play. Not only
would this maximize wealth, it would also maximize utility if we determined that a win of two dollars were twice as valuable to us as a loss of
one dollar.

But what if a win of two dollars were only one-and-a-half times as
valuable to us as a loss of one dollar? To determine how to maximize
utility then, we assign a util value of −1 to the losing scenario, the tails
scenario, and a utils value of 1.5 to the winning scenario, the heads sce-

nario. Now, we determine the optimal f based upon these utils rather than dollars, and we find it to be .166666, or to bet 16⅔% on each and every play to maximize our geometric average utility. That means we divide our total cumulative utils to this point by .166666 to determine the number of contracts.

We can then translate this into how many contracts we have per dollars in our account, and, from there, figure what the f value (between zero and one) is that we are really using (based on dollars, not utils).

If we do this, then the original two-to-one coin toss curve of wealth maximization, which peaks at .25 (Figure 1.2), still applies, and we are at the .166666 f abscissa. Thus, we pay the consequences of being suboptimal in terms of f on our wealth. However, there is a second f curve—one based on our utility—which peaks at .166666, and we are at the optimal f on this curve. Notice that, if we were to accept the .25 optimal f on this curve, we would be way right of the peak and would pay the concomitant consequences of being right of the peak with respect to our utility.

Now, suppose we were profitable in this holding period, and we go in and update the outcomes of the scenarios based on utils, only this time, since we have more wealth, the utility of a winning scenario in the next holding period is only 1.4 utils. Again, we would find our optimal f based on utils. Again, once we determined how many units to trade in the next holding period based on our cumulative utils, we could translate it into what the f (between zero and one) is for dollars, and we would find it to be nonuniform from the previous holding period.

The example shown is one in which we assume a sequence of more than one play, where we are reusing the same money we started with. If there was only one play, one holding period, or we received new money to play at each holding period, maximizing the arithmetic expected utility would be the optimal strategy. However, in most cases we must reuse the money on the next play, the next holding period, that we have used on this last play, and, therefore, we must strive to maximize geometric expected growth. To some, this might mean maximizing the geometric expected growth of wealth; to others, the geometric expected growth of utility. The mathematics is the same for both. Both have two curves in $n + 1$ space: a wealth maximization curve and a utility maximization curve. For those maximizing the expected growth of wealth, the two are the same.

At this point, I reiterate what was said in the beginning of this chapter regarding whether you're in this for anything other than money. This is the wrong place for entertainment, or to try to prove something to yourself or someone else. If you are investing for any other reason than wealth maximization, you will be inclined to make allocations decisions that will cost you money.

Throughout the sequel, we will assume that the reader strives to maximize wealth. However, if the reader has a different utility preference curve other than ln x (wealth maximization), he may apply the techniques herein, provided he substitutes a *utils* quantity for the outcome of each scenario rather than a monetary value, which will then yield a nonuniform optimal f value (one whose value changes from one holding period to the next).

Such readers are forewarned, however, that they will still pay the consequences, in terms of their wealth, for being suboptimal in the $n + 1$ dimensional leverage space of wealth maximization. Again, this is so because, regardless of your utility preference curve, you are somewhere in the leverage space of Figure 1.2 for individual games, and somewhere in the $n + 1$ dimensional leverage space for multiple simultaneous games. You reap the benefits of this, as well as pay the consequences, no matter what your utility preference function. Ideally, you will have a utility preference function and it will be ln x.

REFERENCE

1. Richard J. Tewles, Charles V. Harlow, and Herbert L. Stone, *The Commodity Futures Game, Who Wins? Who Loses? Why?* New York: McGraw-Hill Book Company, 1977.

3
Conditional Probabilities Involving Correlation

This new framework in asset allocation will require that we work with conditional probabilities. Conditional probabilities are the cornerstone of this new framework. Without being able to discern conditional probabilities, we will be unable to discern optimal allocations. So, what is a conditional probability?

A conditional probability is the probability of an event occurring when another event has occurred, or of two events occurring simultaneously. That is to say, what is the probability of B occurring given that A has occurred. This is written as $p(A \mid B)$, which means literally "The probability of A occurring given that B has occurred."

Oftentimes, conditional probabilities are also referred to as *joint probabilities*. The mathematics of the two mean the same. However, typically, the term *conditional probabilities* is used to denote probabilities when one of the events is known to have occurred (i.e., it is assumed the events occur in sequence) and *joint probabilities* is used when they occur simultaneously. Throughout this text, however, they will be considered to mean the same thing (since the mathematics is the same); hence, the terms *conditional probabilities* and *joint probabilities* will be used interchangeably.

The probability of either of two events, A and B, occurring is the sum of their individual probabilities minus their conditional probabilities:

$$p(A \text{ or } B) = p(A) + p(B) - p(A \mid B)$$

Which, for two coins, is:

p(heads on coin 1 or heads on coin 2) = p(heads on coin 1)

$$+ \text{p(heads on coin 2)} - \text{p(heads on both)}$$

p(heads on coin 1 or heads on coin 2) = .5 + .5 − .25 = .75

If we flip two coins simultaneously (or one coin in succession twice), we would expect to get at least one head, with a probability of .75.

If events are mutually exclusive—that is, if both cannot occur, meaning that if one occurs the other cannot—then the conditional probability, $p(A \mid B)$, is zero or, vice versa, one, and the formula becomes:

$$p(A \text{ or } B) = p(A) + p(B)$$

For example, if we are tossing a coin with a .5 probability of coming up tails and a .5 probability of heads, then the probability of getting either a head or a tail is .5 + .5 = 1.

An example of how conditional probabilities apply to this new framework is as follows. Suppose we are considering allocating among two stocks, ABC stock and XYZ stock. We will need to know what the probability is of, say, a 2% or more rise in XYZ when we also have a 2% or more rise in ABC:

$$p(XYZ >= 2\% \mid ABC >= 2\%)$$

Or, we may want to know what the probability is of a 2% or more rise in XYZ when there is a 1% or more decline in ABC:

$$p(XYZ >= 2\% \mid ABC <= -1\%)$$

On the surface, this may appear quite simple, and conventional statistics assumes that it is, but only for a very limited type of case. Conventional statistics pertaining to conditional probabilities can solve this problem only in the very limited case where the correlation coefficient between ABC and XYZ is 0.

Suppose we are tossing a coin. The outcome of an individual random event (random in the sense that we do not know the outcome of the event until it has occurred, such as coin tossing) is called, appropriately, a *random variable*. Thus, if we are tossing a coin, the outcome of the toss is a random variable, and, in this case of coin tossing, it can take one of two values: either heads or tails.

Let us assume for a moment that we are tossing two coins. The probability of getting heads when tossing one of the two coins is .5. (We assume these are perfect coins with a .5 probability of heads and, complementarily, a .5 probability of tails.) The probability of tossing heads on both coins is, therefore, .25, which is arrived at by multiplying .5, the probability of tossing heads with one coin, times .5, the probability of tossing heads with the second coin.

This .25 joint probability of tossing heads with both coins can also be shown by the fact that there are four possible outcomes of tossing the two coins (HH, HT, TH, TT), each with equal probability, thus defining the *sample space*. The chance, then, of getting HH is 1 in 4, or .25.

NUMBER OF OCCURRENCES (FREQUENCIES) AND PROBABILITIES

Most frequently, the joint probabilities of two random variables are shown in the form of a table. For example, considering our stream of simultaneous tosses of two coins (HH, TH, HT, TT), we could construct a table to show these four simultaneous events:

Number of Occurrences (Frequencies)

		Coin 1	
		H	T
Coin 2	H	1	1
	T	1	1

Often, the tables are also expressed as probabilities:

Probabilities

		Coin 1	
		H	T
Coin 2	H	.25	.25
	T	.25	.25

We are assuming, and rightly so, that there is not any correlation between the two coins. That is, the outcomes of the two coin tosses are independent of each other. If this were *not* the case, then each of the four possible outcomes (HH, HT, TH, TT) would *not* have an equal probability of occurrence.

We now introduce the notion of *stochastic independence*. When the joint probability of two events equals the product of their individual probabilities (such as in our coin toss example), then there is said to be stochastic independence. Formally, when

$$p(B|A) = p(A) * p(B) \qquad [3.01]$$

is true, there is stochastic independence. Often, this is referred to as the joint probability of *independent random variables*.

Stochastic independence is, therefore, synonymous, in the sense in which we are using it, with a correlation coefficient of 0 between two streams of outcomes.

We can, therefore, say that if there is stochastic independence, the correlation coefficient is 0. However, the reverse is not true. We will see shortly that it is possible to have a correlation coefficient of 0, yet there is not stochastic independence.

When we speak of a table of outcomes of one random variable, we are referring to what is called the *marginal density* of that variable. For example:

Coin 1

H	T
.5	.5

When we speak of a table of outcomes of more than one variable, we are referring to what is called the *joint density* of the variables. For example:

Coin 1

		H	T
	H	.25	.25
Coin 2			
	T	.25	.25

Traditionally, conditional probabilities were looked at assuming stochastic independence. In many cases, such as tossing two coins, this is a valid assumption. However, in many real-life cases, such as the probability that two stocks will both advance on a given day (since stocks tend to be positively correlated with each other; i.e., the correlation coefficient is >0), the traditional notion doesn't work. The joint probabilities cannot be discerned simply by multiplying together the individual probabilities.

For three years, I was tormented by this problem. I was trying to find the solution to a generalized theory on conditional probabilities. That is, a theory that would explain conditional probabilities for all values of the correlation coefficient, not just for convenient values like 0, 1, or −1. I wanted—I needed—a theory to give me conditional probabilities for *all* values of the correlation coefficient between two random variables.

I hounded universities, math Ph.D.s, nutty professors, South American witch doctors, actuaries, and anyone who I thought might have a clue to answering this problem. For hours, I sifted through mountains of arid technical journals.

I worked on the solution myself, over and over. I tinkered with the notion of superimposing the two distributions of outcomes at angles to themselves based on the correlation coefficient, then taking the double integrals of the surface areas created. I thought for a long time that I could use rulers (partially clear at the probabilities desired and the rest opaque), align them at angles corresponding to their correlation, then shoot light rays which would pass through the clear parts, and the areas intersected by such would be divided by the parallelogram created by the possible areas of intersection to derive the joint probabilities. I had all the calculations derived and programmed into enormous spreadsheets to replicate these conceptual acrobatics. Page after page of notes on legal pads, napkins, and matchbook covers.

The more I worked on the problem, the more necessary the solution seemed. How could no one have the answer to this problem of joint probabilities, which was so necessary to real-life needs? How could conditional probabilities be worked out only for very convenient values of the correlation coefficient? This was the only thing missing from this new framework in asset allocation. I had the objective function worked out, but the objective function called for these conditional probabilities as inputs.

As you will see in the next chapter, everything was worked out for a superior method of asset allocation, except for the ability to discern joint probabilities for all values of the correlation coefficient between two streams of random variables.

The real insult to me was the accepted theorem of conditional probabilities, which was: *joint densities cannot be discerned from their component marginal densities.* The conventional notion assumes that, unless there is stochastic independence, the joint probability density function is a unique, different distribution altogether, as though it just jumps into existence out of nowhere! That is, it is not a function of the component marginal density functions, but it is a new probability density function all its own, which cannot be re-created from the component marginal density functions. To see this, consider the following table taken from Feller and refer to Figure 3.1:[1]

		X				Marginal Density Y
		0	1	2	3	
Y	1	2	0	0	1	3
	2	6	6	6	0	18
	3	0	6	0	0	6
Marginal Density X		8	12	6	1	27

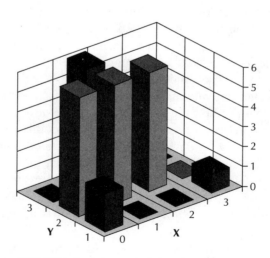

FIGURE 3.1   Joint probability distributions.

The correlation coefficient between the streams of event X and event Y is 0. Therefore, we would expect the probabilities at $X = 0$, $Y = 3$ to be $(6/27)*(8/27)$ or $.222 * .2963 = .0658$ if there was stochastic independence. Instead, the probability is zero, thus confirming the accepted theorem of conditional probabilities that joint densities cannot be discerned from their component marginal densities.

Now, it is possible to determine a correlation coefficient given only the joint density and the marginal densities,[2] but it has long been regarded that you cannot determine the joint density given only the marginal densities and their correlation coefficient, which is exactly what I needed.

I could not accept the conventional notion and became ever more obsessed with finding an answer to this problem that would be clean and easy to employ. That is, I wanted an answer whereby, given the correlation coefficient and the probabilities associated with two scenario spectrums (e.g., two coins which have two scenarios, H and T, with probabilities .5 and .5, respectively), representing two marginal probability densities, one could figure out the joint probability density.

I've finally figured out the mechanics of how it works, how joint probability densities are formed from marginal probability densities. However, as you shall see, the mechanics are not as clean and easy as I would have liked.

Again, nature refuses to cooperate.

Now, we will consider two simultaneous scenario spectrums in which there is a correlation coefficient between them, and discern the joint probabilities of two prescribed scenarios, one from each spectrum, occurring.

Consider, now, when we toss two coins and they have stochastic independence between them (i.e., the linear correlation coefficient r is 0), the probability of both landing heads up is the product of individual probabilities (see Equation [3.01]):

$$p(H_1 \mid H_2) = p(H_1) * p(H_2)$$

or, the more shorthanded form:

$$P_{(1 \mid 2)} = P_1 * P_2$$

Now, let us imagine that the two coins can communicate telepathically so that when the first coin comes up heads, the second coin also comes up heads. This would correspond to a linear correlation coefficient r of 1. The probability of getting both heads is .5, the probability of getting heads on the toss of coin 1.

If the correlation coefficient were -1 (that is, when the first coin landed heads, the second coin always landed tails), then the probability of tossing both coins and having them both come up heads would be zero. However, the probability of having the first coin come up heads and the second coin come up tails is .5, equal to the probability of the first coin coming up heads (since, when $r = -1$, the second coin always comes up tails when the first coin comes up heads).

We introduce now the notion of *interantisection,* for lack of a better term (and to further avoid Greek letters as variables). Reconsider the case in which $r = 1$, that is, when one coin lands heads, the other coin also lands heads. We say the probability of this is .5, equal to the probability of one of the coins coming up heads, since we are using perfect coins with a .5 probability of coming up heads.

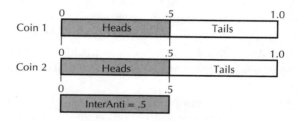

Suppose, however, that one of the coins is not perfect, and rather than a .5 probability of coming up heads, the probability is .4. Now, the probability of both coming up heads is .4, the lower of the two probabilities that overlap.

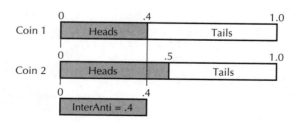

If the probability of getting tails were .4 (and thus the probability of getting heads would be .6), then the probability of both coming up heads is

.5, the lower of the two probabilities (i.e., since you have a .6 probability on one coin and a .5 probability on the other).

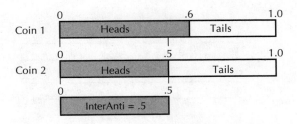

It doesn't matter which coin, the first or the second, has the lower probability:

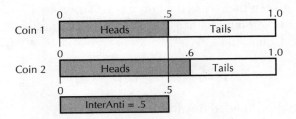

The interantisection is the overlap when $r = 1$, and, thus, it is the lower of the two probabilities. In the preceding figure, the interantisection of both coins coming up tails would be .4. In other words, *when r is positive, the interantisection is the intersection of the two probabilities.*

When the correlation coefficient is negative, the second scenario spectrum (coin 2, in this case) is turned around (flipped) 180 degrees.

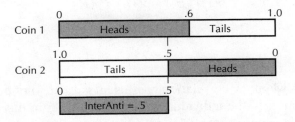

Notice how coin two is flipped 180 degrees in the previous illustration, thus showing the joint probability of .5 getting a head with the first coin (with a probability of .6) and a tail with the second (with a probability) of .5 when the correlation coefficient between the two coins is –1.

If, in the previous example, we wished to find the interantisection of both coming up heads, the probability would be .1, as depicted in the next illustration:

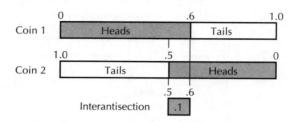

Recall now when we toss two coins, and they have stochastic independence between them (i.e., the linear correlation coefficient r is 0), the probability of both landing heads is the product of individual probabilities (refer to Equation [3.01]):

$$p(H_1 \mid H_2) = p(H_1) * p(H_2)$$

or, the more shorthanded form:

$$p_{(1 \mid 2)} = p_1 * p_2$$

Therefore, the probability of getting both coins to land heads, when the correlation coefficient between them is 0, and they are perfect coins (i.e., each has a .5 probability of landing heads), is:

$$p(H_1 \mid H_2) = p(H_1) * p(H_2)$$

$$= .5 * .5$$

$$= .25$$

However, when the correlation coefficient is 1, the joint probability is the intersection of the individual probabilities, or .5 in this case. When the correlation coefficient is −1, it is the intersection after flipping one of the scenario spectrums around 180 degrees (the antisection), or in this case, it would be 0 probability of both coming up heads.

So, we can find joint probabilities when the correlation coefficient between two scenario spectrums is −1, 0, or 1. How, then, do we approximate joint probabilities when the correlation coefficient is not at such convenient values?

Notice that there are two factors affecting joint probabilities. The first of these is the product of the individual probabilities (when r is 0):

$$p_1 * p_2$$

The second of these is the interantisection of the two probabilities (when $|r| = 1$):

$$I(p_1, p_2)$$

In joint probabilities, the lower limit is zero probability, as either the interantisection can be 0, or, if p_1 or p_2 is 0, then both the first factor, the product of the two probabilities, and the second factor, their interantisection, will be 0.

The upper limit that a joint probability can be is the lesser of p_1 or p_2. This can be shown since the interantisection factor can never be greater than the minimum of p_1 or p_2, and, since the highest a probability can be is 1, then the product of $p_1 * p_2$ can never be greater than the lesser of p_1 or p_2. Thus, we can state that the upper limit on a joint probability is the lesser of the two probabilities.

A conditional probability is a *linearly weighted sum of the two factors,* in light of the lower limit of 0 probability and the upper limit of the minimum of p_1 and p_2 that confines our answer:

$$p_1 * p_2 * \text{Weight1}$$

$$+$$

$$I(p_1, p_2) * \text{Weight2}$$

And what do we use as the weights? As it turns out, weight1 is 1 minus the absolute value of the correlation coefficient:

$$\text{Weight1} = (1 - |r|)$$

And weight2 is simply the absolute value of the correlation coefficient:

$$\text{Weight2} = |r|$$

This weighting scheme insures that we will be within the upper and lower limit, inclusive. Thus, when $r = 0$, the equation is weighted completely in favor of the product of the two probabilities, and when $|r| = 1$, the weighting is completely in favor of the interantisection. The complete equation for approximating joint probabilities, then, is:

$$p(p_1 \mid p_2) = p_1 * p_2 * (1 - |r|) + I(p_1, p_2) * |r| \qquad [3.02]$$

We say that the function is linearly weighted (i.e., none of the terms has an exponent greater than 1) because a linear function graphs as a straight line. We can see that the relationship between $p_1 * p_2$ and $I(p_1, p_2)$ is linear by considering the following two streams of coin tosses

Stream 1   H   H   H   H   H   T   T   T   T   T

Stream 2   H   H   H   H   T   H   T   T   T   T

TIME ⟶

If we look at the two streams, we see that there is a .5 probability of the outcome H in each stream, and a .5 probability of the outcome T in each stream. If we calculate the correlation coefficient between the two streams, we find it to be .6.

Now, we find $p_1 * p_2$ to be $.5 * .5 = .25$, corresponding to an r of 0. We can further find the interantisection $I(p_1, p_2)$ to be .5 if we are looking at getting heads in both streams simultaneously:

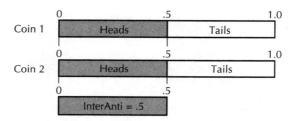

Since the correlation coefficient is greater than 0, we do not flip the second scenario spectrum 180 degrees. Notice that if we were looking at the interantisection of both streams coming up tails simultaneously, we would have an interantisection of .5 as well.

Now, we have $p_1 * p_2$ equal to .25, the joint probability of both coming up heads (or, in this case, both tails as well) at $r = 0$. At $r = 1$ we have the

joint probability equal to the interantisection of .5. At $r = -1$, we would
have an interantisection of 0, thus a probability of 0, as depicted here:

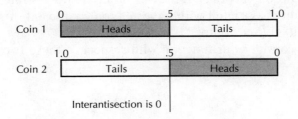

Interantisection is 0

Thus, we have the following three points of which we are certain:

r	Probability
−1	0
0	.25
1	.5

Plotting these values on a graph, we can see the three points in Figure 3.2.

We can see that the three points *could* be connected by a straight line.
However, they could also be connected by a curved line (i.e., the function would not be linearly weighted), such as a sigmoid function (i.e., a
stretched out S shape connecting the three points).

We can see, however, that heads comes up in both streams four of the
ten times (likewise, tails comes up in both streams four of the ten times)

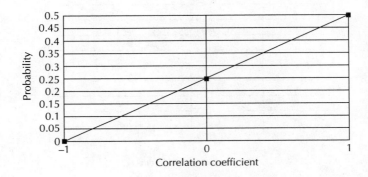

FIGURE 3.2

for a probability of .4. Notice that if the function is linear—that is, if the function is a straight line—then the line at a correlation coefficient of .6 crosses at a probability of .4. If the function were not a straight line, then the probability associated with a correlation coefficient of .6 would be anything but .4! (See Figure 3.3.)

Now, we consider our function with respect to these two streams of outcomes:

$$p_{(1\,|\,2)} = p_1 * p_2 * (1 - |r|) + I(p_1, p_2) * |r|$$

$$= .5 * .5 * (1 - |.6|) + .5 * |.6|$$

$$= .25 * .4 + .5 * .6$$

$$= .1 + .3$$

$$= .4$$

Thus, we can see that our formula gives us an answer which is confirmed simply by examining the stream of outcomes. We can expect heads to come up in both streams simultaneously with a probability of .4 when two perfect coins are tossed which have a .6 correlation between them.

This is an approximation which holds only for binomial distributions (i.e., two scenarios in a spectrum). The further the probabilities get from .5 of the scenarios, the less accurate this becomes. In other words, the solution is exact when you dichotomize two scenario spectrums; otherwise, it becomes an approximation of diminishing accuracy.

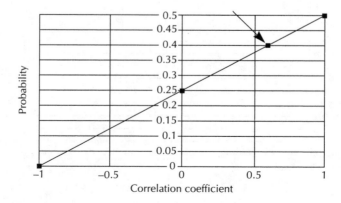

FIGURE 3.3   Joint probabilities are linearly weighted by the correlation coefficient.

However, all scenario spectrums can be turned into binomial distributions (set to just two scenarios), by dichotomizing them near their centers. Again consider the XYZ Manufacturing scenario spectrum. In it we have five different scenarios. We could dichotomize it by lumping the War, Trouble, and Stagnation scenarios into one scenario in the new scenario spectrum, which we will call the *Bad Half of Outcomes* scenario. Likewise, we can lump the peace and prosperity scenarios into the *Good Half of Outcomes* scenario in the converted spectrum. Now, we can compare our converted spectrum with other spectrums that have two scenarios in it to approximate joint probabilities between the four possible joint outcomes (Figure 3.4).

Dichotomizing scenario spectrums to approximate joint probabilities is a valid exercise, so long as you dichotomize the scenario spectrums near the .5 probability levels. The further you dichotomize from there, the less accurate the approximation.

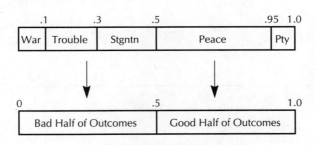

FIGURE 3.4

Returning to the Feller example taken from earlier in this chapter:

		X				
		0	1	2	3	Marginal Density Y
	1	2	0	0	1	3
Y	2	6	6	6	0	18
	3	0	6	0	0	6
Marginal Density X		8	12	6	1	27

If we dichotomize the X scenario spectrum, lumping outcomes 0 and 1 into what we'll call scenario A in the X spectrum, and outcomes 2 and 3 into what we'll call scenario B in the X spectrum, we will not have dichotomized X at the .5 level; we will have dichotomized it at the .74074 level, because, looking at the marginal density for X, twenty of the twenty-seven outcomes (74.074%) are at 1 or 2, and only seven of the twenty-seven outcomes (25.92%) are at 2 or 3. (See Figure 3.5.)

Now, if we do the same with scenario spectrum Y, lumping outcomes 1 and 2 into what we'll call scenario A in the Y spectrum, and scenario outcome 3 will be called scenario B in the Y spectrum, we convert the Y spectrum as shown in Figure 3.6.

Notice that the Y spectrum, too, is not dichotomized at the .5 level, but rather is dichotomized at the .777 level.

Now, we can begin to create a table of joint probabilities as follows:

		X		
		A	B	Marginal Density Y
Y	A	?	?	.777
	B	?	?	.222
Marginal Density X		.74074	.2592	1.0

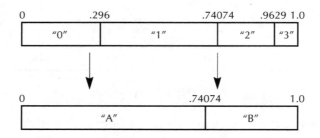

FIGURE 3.5 X marginal density dichotomization.

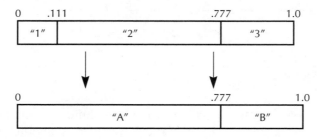

FIGURE 3.6 Y marginal density dichotomization.

Now, bearing in mind that the correlation coefficient r between these two scenario spectrums is 0, we determine the four joint probabilities of the table:

$$p(A \mid A) = .74074 * .777 * (1 - 0) + .74074 * 0$$

$$= .5761$$

$$p(A \mid B) = .74074 * .222 * (1 - 0) + 0 * 0$$

$$= .16461$$

$$p(B \mid A) = .2592 * .777 * (1 - 0) + .0362 * 0$$

$$= .2016461$$

$$p(B \mid B) = .2592 * .222 * (1 - 0) + .222 * 0$$

$$= .05761316873$$

(Notice the interantisection values in the preceding equations.)
We can now complete the table as:

$$X$$

		A	B
Y	A	.5761	.2016461
	B	.16461	.05761

Since, in the original table, we did not use probabilities, but, rather, the actual counts of twenty-seven events, we can multiply twenty-seven by each of these probabilities to obtain the frequency expectations of the table:

$$X$$

		A	B
Y	A	15.56	5.44
	B	4.44	1.56

We see that we can expect 15.56 events (of the twenty-seven) to occur, getting scenario A in spectrum X and scenario A in spectrum Y. Recall that this corresponds to getting a 0 or a 1 in the original spectrum X, and a 1 or a 2 in the original spectrum Y. We can see from the original spectrum that there were actually fourteen such occurrences of the twenty-seven:

		X				
		0	1	2	3	Marginal Density Y
	1	2	0	0	1	3
Y	2	6	6	6	0	18
	3	0	6	0	0	6
Marginal Density X		8	12	6	1	27

Similar errors can be found in the other three quadrants. The reason for the inexactitude is that we dichotomized the original distribution too far from the actual .5 probability midpoints (we dichotomized at .74074 and .777). Thus, our approximations of the joint probabilities became less accurate.

Let's go back and dichotomize this table at the .5 levels. To do this, we ask ourselves, "Where does the .5 probability fall on the X axis?"

First, we take the sum of each X outcome times its frequency:

$$8 * 2 = 0$$

$$12 * 1 = 12$$

$$6 * 2 = 12$$

$$1 * 3 = 3$$

$$\text{Sum} = 27$$

Then we divide this sum by 27, the total number of occurrences, to obtain a probability weighted average (which occurs at the .5 percentile)

$$\frac{27}{27} = 1$$

Thus, if this were a continuous distribution, we would expect 50% of the values to be below 1 and 50% above.

$$1 * 3 = 3$$

$$2 * 18 = 36$$

$$3 * 6 = 18$$

$$\text{Sum} = 57$$

Then, we divide this sum by 27, the total number of occurrences, to obtain a probability weighted average (which occurs at the .5 percentile)

$$\frac{57}{27} = 2.111$$

Thus, if this were a continuous distribution, we would expect 50% of the values to be below 2.111 and 50% above.

Now, we calculate the probabilities for the four quadrants as:

$$p(<.5 \mid <.5) = .5 * .5 * (1 - |0|) + .5 * |0|$$

$$= .25 * 1 + .5 * 0$$

$$= .25$$

"Wait a second," you say, "Since there is stochastic independence here, we need not go through this exercise; we can simply multiply the probabilities together for each of the four quadrants to determine the probabilities associated with each quadrant. This works out to a joint probability of .25 for each quadrant." All of this is absolutely correct. The quadrants are split right at the X value of 1, and right at the Y value of 2.111. Thus, we would expect 25%, or 6.75 (27 * .25) occurrences in each quadrant.

Looking at the table, it may be a little difficult to discern 6.75 outcomes in each quadrant, since the table represents discrete outcomes, and we are treating it as though they are continuous for the sake of dichotomizing the table conveniently at the .5 probability levels. For example, looking at the table, the row of Y values for the "2" outcome, how many of these are above and how many below the 2.111 level?

Naturally, it is easier to see how the mechanics of deriving joint distributions from the component marginal distributions works, by using more convenient marginal distributions.

Now, we will consider another case of two streams of outcomes over twelve plays:

Stream X	2	1	−1	−2	2	1	−1	−2	2	1	−1	−2
Stream Y	2	2	2	1	1	1	−1	−1	−1	−2	−2	−2

TIME $\longrightarrow$

We can determine the correlation coefficient r between these two streams as .33333. Now, if we set out to construct a joint probabilities table, we can see the marginal densities as well (each of the four possible scenarios in each scenario spectrum has exactly a .25 probability of occurrence).

		X				
		−2	−1	1	2	Marginal Density Y
	−2	1	1	1	0	3 (p = .25)
Y	−1	1	1	0	1	3 (p = .25)
	1	1	0	1	1	3 (p = .25)
	2	0	1	1	1	3 (p = .25)
Marginal Density X		3	3	3	3	12
or probability of		.25	.25	.25	.25	p = 1.0

Now, if we dichotomize exactly at the .5 probability level for both scenario spectrums, we will have two scenarios in each spectrum, which we will call + and −, each with a .5 probability of occurrence. The plus scenarios incorporate those outcomes which were greater than 0, and the minus outcomes incorporate those less than 0. We now have:

		X	
		−	+
Y	−	4	2
	+	2	4

Now, let us go back to our equation for determining joint probabilities, and see how closely we get to arriving at the answers displayed in the following:

$$p(-\,|\,-) = .5 * .5 * (1 - |.3333|) + .5 * |.3333|$$

$$= .25 * .6666 + .5 * .3333$$

$$= .166666 + .166666$$

$$= .33333$$

$$p(-\,|\,+) = .5 * .5 * (1 - |.3333|) + 0 * |.3333|$$

$$= .25 * .6666 + 0$$

$$= .166666 + 0$$

$$= .166666$$

$$p(+\mid+) = .5 * .5 * (1 - |.3333|) + .5 * |.3333|$$
$$= .25 * .6666 + .5 * .3333$$
$$= .166666 + .166666$$
$$= .33333$$

$$p(+\mid-) = .5 * .5 * (1 - |.3333|) + 0 * |.3333|$$
$$= .25 * .6666 + 0$$
$$= .166666 + 0$$
$$= .166666$$

Thus, our formula approximates the joint probabilities to be:

X

		$-$	$+$
Y	$-$	.333333	.1666666
	$+$	.166666	.3333333

If we multiply the probabilities by the number of outcomes (12), we get the following expected table of outcomes:

X

		$-$	$+$
Y	$-$	4	2
	$+$	2	4

Which is exactly what the empirical data, the stream of outcomes, did. Notice our answer is exact because we dichotomized at the .5 levels.

From this table, for instance, we would expect a negative number in Stream X and a negative number in Stream Y for four of the twelve times, and so on through the other three quadrants.

"But wait," you say, "Can't we take one of these four quadrants, and dichotomize it to determine the probabilities to a finer degree than simply this?" In other words, you don't simply want to know, from the previous example, what the probability is of getting, say, a positive number in both streams. You may want to know what the probability is of getting a −2 in Stream X and a −1 in Stream Y. What has been discussed thus far will give you the exact joint distribution when you have two binary marginal distributions—that is, when you have marginal distributions that both have only two possible outcomes, two possible scenarios (like most gambling situations, where you win M with X probability or lose N with Y probability). However, we wish to discern joint distributions when the marginal distributions are of any variety, not just binary.

This brings us to the heart of the matter.

A THEORY OF CONDITIONAL PROBABILITY

We can dichotomize the table of joint probabilities between any two scenario spectrums given only the scenario spectrums themselves (i.e., the probability associated with each scenario) and the correlation coefficient between the two scenario spectrums. Thus, we can determine what the probabilities are for each of the four quadrants of a table of joint probabilities.

We can further dichotomize the table to obtain probabilities to a greater precision than just four quadrants of the table. That is, we can take, say, the upper-left quadrant of a table, and use that as a table in itself. Doing this with all four quadrants would give us four quadrants within each of the original four quadrants. Thus, we would have joint probabilities for each of the sixteen sections of a table. We could continue to as great a level of precision as desired.

There is one catch, though, and it is the very heart of conditional probabilities involving correlation itself. That is, **each quadrant has its very own correlation coefficient.** To see this, let's return to our previous example. We start out with the following stream of outcomes:

Stream X	2	1	−1	−2	2	1	−1	−2	2	1	−1	−2
Stream Y	2	2	2	1	1	1	−1	−1	−1	−2	−2	−2

$$\text{TIME} \longrightarrow$$

Thus, we can create the following table:

$$X$$

		−2	−1	1	2	Marginal Density Y
	−2	1	1	1	0	3 (p = .25)
Y	−1	1	1	0	1	3 (p = .25)
	1	1	0	1	1	3 (p = .25)
	2	0	1	1	1	3 (p = .25)
Marginal Density X		3	3	3	3	12

We know that the correlation coefficient r between these two streams is .33333. However, this correlation coefficient applies only to the first quadrant, which is the entire table.

Now, using our equation for determining joint probabilities involving correlation for dichotomized scenario spectrums, we discern the joint probabilities for all four quadrants of the table as:

X

		−	+
Y	−	.333333	.1666666
	+	.166666	.3333333

If we multiply the probabilities by the number of outcomes (12), we get the following table of frequencies of expected outcomes:

X

		−	+
Y	−	4	2
	+	2	4

Now we can state that the −,− quadrant, that is, the upper-left quadrant, is a table which we would like to dichotomize. That is, we want to know the joint probabilities associated between X and Y when both X and Y are negative:

X

		−2	−1
Y	−2	?	?
	−1	?	?

However, the theory of conditional probabilities involving correlation tells us that we cannot use the correlation coefficient for the entire distribution (which we know is .333). Instead, we must use the correlation coefficient of only those outcomes where both X and Y are negative. Thus, we use only those snippets of the streams of outcomes where both outcomes are negative, and we obtain:

Stream X −1 −2 −1 −2
Stream Y −1 −1 −2 −2
TIME ⟶

Taking the correlation coefficient between these two streams, we find it to be 0. Also, notice that the probability of a −1 or a −2 in either of these two streams is .5; we must use .5 for the individual probabilities. Thus, we have the following joint probabilities:

$$p(-2 \mid -2) = .5 * .5 * (1 - |0|) + .5 * 0$$
$$= .25 * 1 + .5 * 0$$
$$= .25$$

Thus, .25 of the upper-left quadrant should be −2,−2, and since .3333 of the entire distribution is in the upper-left quadrant, we would expect .25 * .3333, or .08333 of the distribution to be at −2,−2.

$$p(-2 \mid -1) = .5 * .5 * (1 - |0|) + .5 * 0$$
$$= .25 * 1 + .5 * 0$$
$$= .25$$

Thus, .25 of the upper-left quadrant should be −2,−1, and since .3333 of the entire distribution is in the upper-left quadrant, we would expect .25 * .3333, or .08333 of the distribution to be at −2,−1.

$$p(-1 \mid -2) = .5 * .5 * (1 - |0|) + .5 * 0$$
$$= .25 * 1 + .5 * 0$$
$$= .25$$

Thus, .25 of the upper-left quadrant should be −1,−2, and since .3333 of the entire distribution is in the upper-left quadrant, we would expect .25 * .3333, or .08333 of the distribution to be at −1,−2.

$$p(-1 \mid -1) = .5 * .5 * (1 - |0|) + .5 * 0$$
$$= .25 * 1 + .5 * 0$$
$$= .25$$

Thus, .25 of the upper-left quadrant should be −1,−1, and since .3333 of the entire distribution is in the upper-left quadrant, we would expect .25 * .3333, or .08333 of the distribution to be at −1,−1.

$$X$$

		-2	-1
Y	-2	.0833	.0833
	-1	.0833	.0833

Recall that there were 12 outcomes in the initial streams and table. Multiplying the probabilities (.083333) by 12 gives us 1. Thus, our table of expected frequencies of outcomes appears as:

$$X$$

		-2	-1
Y	-2	1	1
	-1	1	1

Notice that this is exactly the same as the upper-left quadrant of the table taken from the actual streams.

The lower-right quadrant could be solved in a similar fashion. However, let's look at the lower-left quadrant (and, the upper-right quadrant could be solved in a fashion similar to how we are about to solve the lower-left).

Stream X -1 -2

Stream Y 2   1

The correlation coefficient is 1. The probability of getting a -1 or a -2 in Stream X is .5, as is the probability associated with getting a 1 or a 2 in Stream Y. Thus, we have the following joint probabilities:

$$p(-2 \mid 1) = .5 * .5 * (1 - |1|) + .5 * 1$$
$$= .25 * 0 + .5 * 1$$
$$= .5$$

Thus, .5 of the lower-left quadrant should be $-2,1$, and since .16666 of the entire distribution is in the lower-left quadrant, we would expect .5 * .16666, or .08333 of the distribution to be at $-2,1$.

$$p(-2 \mid 2) = .5 * .5 * (1 - |1|) + 0 * 1$$
$$= .25 * 0 + 0 * 1$$
$$= 0$$

Thus, 0 of the lower-left quadrant should be −2,2, and since .16666 of the entire distribution is in the lower-left quadrant, we would expect .0 * .16666, or .0 of the distribution to be at −2,2.

$$p(-1 \mid 1) = .5 * .5 * (1 - |1|) + 0 * 1$$
$$= .25 * 0 + 0 * 1$$
$$= 0$$

Thus, 0 of the lower-left quadrant should be −1,1, and since .16666 of the entire distribution is in the lower-left quadrant, we would expect 0 * .16666, or .0 of the distribution to be at −1,1.

$$p(-1 \mid 2) = .5 * .5 * (1 - |1|) + .5 * 1$$
$$= .25 * 0 + .5 * 1$$
$$= .5$$

Thus, .5 of the lower-left quadrant should be −1,2, and since .16666 of the entire distribution is in the lower-left quadrant, we would expect .5 * .16666, or .08333 of the distribution to be at −1,2. Thus, the lower-left quadrant can be further dichotomized to be:

X

		−2	−1
Y	−2	.0833	0
	−1	0	.0833

Which, multiplying the probabilities by 12, the total number of out-comes in the original streams, we would get the following expectations:

X

		−2	−1
Y	−2	1	0
	−1	0	1

Notice that this is exactly the way the table constructed from the original streams appeared.

Thus, you can dichotomize scenario spectrums, and, applying the formula, derive conditional probabilities involving correlation. The difficulty is that, rather than being able to use the single correlation coefficient of the entire table, you must use the correlation coefficient unique to those outcomes for the subtable you are creating.

Let's consider one more example. Suppose we flip three dimes and three quarters. We will say that scenario spectrum A is the total number of heads of the six coins, and scenario spectrum B is the total number of heads of the quarters only. The joint probability table will appear as such:

		\multicolumn{7}{c}{A}	
		0	1	2	3	4	5	6	Marginal Density B
B	0	1	3	3	1	0	0	0	8
	1	0	3	9	9	3	0	0	24
	2	0	0	3	9	9	3	0	24
	3	0	0	0	1	3	3	1	8
Marginal Density A		1	6	15	20	15	6	13	64

Altogether there are 2^6 (64) possible outcomes, and the correlation coefficient is .707 (Figure 3.7). Thus, if we want to determine the joint

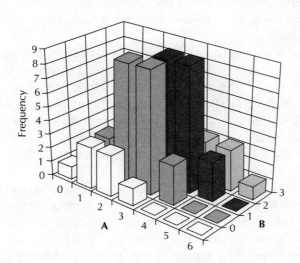

FIGURE 3.7 Joint distribution example of tossing three dimes and three quarters.

probability associated with $A <= 2$ and $B <= 1$ (i.e., the probability, in flipping three dimes and three quarters, of having two or less heads in the six coins and one or less heads in the quarters):

$$p(<= 2 \mid <= 1) = ((15 + 6 + 1)/64) * ((8 + 24)/64) * (1 - |.707|)$$

$$+ ((15 + 6 + 1)/64) * |.707|$$

$$= (22/64) * (32/64) * .293 + (22/64) * .707$$

$$= .34375 * .5 * .293 + .37375 * .707$$

$$= .050359375 + .26424125$$

$$= .314600625$$

Which, when multiplied by 64 (the total number of outcomes), yields an expectation of 20.1344 outcomes in this quadrant. We find there are 19 outcomes in this quadrant.

Notice that although we dichotomized B at the .5 level, we did not dichotomize A there as well, hence the discrepancy between our results and the empirical data. However, if we could have dichotomized along A at .5 as well, our results would have been completely accurate.

Once we have dichotomized a table, we can take one of the new sections and dichotomize it, *provided we know the correlation coefficient of that new table.*

Thus, if we now wanted to dichotomize this upper-left quadrant of this table, we could not use .707 as the correlation coefficient. We would have to determine (or estimate) the correlation coefficient for only that data set where, in flipping three dimes and three quarters, we get two or less heads in the six coins and one or less heads in the quarters.

So, given two scenario spectrums and the correlation coefficient(s) between them, we can discern the joint probabilities of two scenarios occurring, one from each spectrum.

Practitioners of mean-variance, the old framework, have essentially been working with joint distributions that have four quadrants only, by the nature of employing the correlation coefficient to measure the relationships of components. This is a poor proxy for the actual joint distribution, and one more reason this new framework is superior to the old.

JOINT PROBABILITIES BETWEEN TWO CONTINUOUS DISTRIBUTIONS

The scenario spectrums can also be thought of as *binned* distributions, or discrete distributions. **We can use the same technique to discern probabilities from continuous distributions,** if we consider that a continuous distribution is the same as a discrete distribution with infinitely small bins (i.e., infinitely many scenarios).

For example, we know that in the normal distribution, there is a .9772 probability that an observed random variable will fall shy of two standard deviations. There is a .9986 probability that a normally distributed random variable will fall shy of three standard deviations. If we have a scenario that calls for a normally distributed random variable to be between +2 and +3 standard units, as one scenario in a spectrum, we then know that the probability of this scenario is .0214 (.9986 − .9772). We can then discern joint probabilities from continuous distributions. Also, we can make the scenarios as tiny as we like. In the previously cited example, we could have used a scenario which called for a normally distributed random variable to fall between +2 and +2.1 standard units, or between +2 and +2.000001 standard units.

ESTIMATING JOINT PROBABILITIES

The theory presented herein, that all joint probability distributions can be estimated into quarters when you know the marginal densities and the correlation coefficient among the marginal densities, is quite fascinating. It accurately describes the mechanics of constructing a joint distribution from the component marginal distributions. If we are simply using Bernoulli distributions (distributions with only two possible outcomes, i.e., scenario spectrums consisting of only two scenarios) we can get a very good, quick handle on the joint probabilities. However, to cut it finer than this, to find joint probabilities to a greater degree than simply quarters requires knowing the correlation coefficients of the other quarters (or so on) in advance (or, knowing the joint probabilities in advance so you can, by reversing the equation, determine the correlation coefficients).

When dependency is present, the joint distributions are different, depending upon the outcome(s) immediately prior.

Often, we will not know all of the correlation coefficients between two scenario spectrums, and we, therefore, will have to obtain the data, either empirically or through estimation.

Obtaining joint probabilities empirically is really quite simple, if you have the empirical data. For example, suppose we are looking at joint probabilities between two stocks, XYZ Corporation and ABC Corporation. We have numerous different scenarios for what we expect the price of each to do over the next holding period (and a holding period can be any uniform length we choose—it can be a day, two days, a week, month, year, whatever). We have one scenario in the ABC spectrum calling for ABC to be up two points. We also have a scenario in the XYZ spectrum calling for XYZ to be down one-half point. (We can also use percentages if we like, we need not use raw point values.) Now, we can have the computer comb through the price data for both of these stocks and tell us how many holding periods saw ABC up two and XYZ down one-half, then divide the total by the total number of holding periods in the data. Then, we could do that for every combination of two scenarios between the two spectrums. Thus, we would have empirically derived a joint probability table between the two scenario spectrums.

Of course, if you have the empirical data at hand, rather than going in and empirically deriving the probabilities, you can empirically derive the needed correlation coefficients. From there, you can then construct a table of joint probabilities.

We can also estimate the probabilities, in the table of joint probabilities, between the two scenario spectrums. In doing so, we must bear in mind the upper and lower limits of each joint probability, and make sure our estimate does not exceed these limits. The lower limit in a joint probability, you'll recall, is 0. The upper limit is the lower of the two individual probabilities.

You must also have the sum of all the joint probability cells in the table equal to 1.0 exactly.

Also, remember that each row and each column, in a joint probability table between two scenario spectrums, must total the marginal density for that row or column. For example, consider two different scenario spectrums:

Spectrum Y

Scenario	Probability
Good Outcomes	.4
Bad Outcomes	.6

Spectrum X

Scenario	Probability
War	.1
Trouble	.2
Stagnation	.2
Peace	.45
Prosperity	.05

Thus, we construct the table:

	Good Outcomes	Bad Outcomes	Marginal Density X
War			.1
Trouble	.		.2
Stagnation			.2
Peace			.45
Prosperity			.05
Marginal Density Y	.4	.6	1.0

From this example, you can see that the sum of the probabilities in the first column must total the marginal density associated with the first column, Good Outcomes, of .4. That is, the sum of the joint probabilities of War, Trouble, Stagnation, Peace, and Prosperity, jointly with Good Outcomes, must total exactly .4.

Likewise, the total of the probabilities in the first row, that is, the joint probabilities between Good Outcomes and War, along with Bad Outcomes and War, must total the probabilities associated with that row, War, of .1. If we were dealing with the last row, Prosperity, the total of the Good Outcomes and Prosperity, along with the Bad Outcomes and Prosperity, must equal .05.

Notice, if you require that the joint probabilities in each row *and* each column equal the marginal densities associated with each row and each column (as you must do), then you need not worry about exceeding the upper limits on any of the joint probabilities (and, so long as all of your joint probabilities are greater than or equal to 0, as they must be, you need not worry about exceeding the lower bound on joint probabilities). Also, if the joint probabilities in each row *and* each column equal the marginal densities associated with each row and each column, then the sum of all the joint probability cells in the table will be equal to 1.0 exactly (assuming the sum of the probabilities of each scenario spectrum equals 1.0 exactly).

Often, if possible, you may wish to employ a combination of both methods in deriving joint probabilities.* Of course, if you can get the necessary correlation coefficients, you can discern the joint probabilities from the formula.

Finally, when you bin empirical data, use the median value of bin as the outcome of that scenario. For example, if you have a bin of $0 to $100 profit, and three values fall in that bin, $10, $20, and $90, use the median value, $20, to represent the outcome of that scenario.

This new model presented in this book, in the next chapter, is mathematically exact. The only inputs it requires are the scenarios, that is, the probability of such and such an outcome. It is the input of estimations of joint (conditional) probabilities that is paramount. If the probabilities are not any good, the output of this new model will not be either. Assigning accurate joint probabilities to the possible outcomes of multiple simultaneous scenario spectrums is the problem. Since getting to the peak of the curve in the n + 1 dimensional landscape is every bit as important as the exercise of timing and trade selection, and, since this new model will give us this peak (or any other point we wish to be at) with accuracy only as good as our estimation of joint probabilities, then we can state that estimating joint probabilities is ultimately every bit as important as the exercise of timing and trade selection. Perhaps even more so, as we have control over our estimates, and we do not have control over whether the next trade will be profitable.

---

* In estimating joint probabilities, you may wish to model the curves formed by the values of the rows and columns in the table by a mathematical process. Perhaps some form of regression analysis, neural networks, or other techniques might help in estimating either these joint probabilities or the correlation coefficients embedded in the joint distribution per the Theory on Conditional Probability presented herein. This is truly a wide-open area. In *The Mathematics of Money Management,* Chapter 4, a technique for modeling a distribution of a single random variable, using the K-S test, was presented. Such a technique can also be used to model the rows and columns of a joint probability table. Those interested in further pursuing similar techniques should learn about *Pearson curves* and also about *Bayesian statistics.* On the latter, I recommend Howard Raiffa and Robert Schlaifer, *Applied Statistical Decision Theory,* Boston: Harvard University, 1961, and Richard Bellman, *Adaptive Control Processes,* Princeton: Princeton University Press, 1961.

REFERENCES

1. William Feller, *An Introduction to Probability Theory and Its Applications,* Vol. II, New York: John Wiley & Sons, 1966.
2. Fred Gehm, *Commodity Market Money Management,* New York: Wiley, 1983, p. 80.

4

A New Model

With conditional probabilities under our belt, along with the material in Chapters 1 and 2, we now have the basis to create a new model. The new asset allocation model to be presented will allow us to view things within the context of the new framework discussed at length in the beginning of the text.

This new model is algorithmic in operation. That is, it does not rely upon using the past raw data. In Chapter 1, an empirical model—one that does rely upon the past raw data—was presented which allows you to construct the topography in $n + 1$ space, if you so desire. However, an algorithmic solution, such as the one to be presented, is desirable, particularly if, in the future, there is an effort to track the movement of the peak of the curve in $n + 1$ space. An empirical solution can not only be very time consuming, it also does not facilitate what-if types of simulations. Furthermore, you can always use past raw data in an algorithmic model if you like (i.e., create scenario spectrums exactly consistent with what was seen historically). However, the reverse is not true.

MATHEMATICAL OPTIMIZATION

Mathematical optimization is an exercise in finding a maximum or minimum value of an objective function for a given parameter(s). The objective function is, thus, something that can only be solved through an iterative procedure.

For example, the process of finding the optimal f for a single market system, or a single scenario spectrum, is an exercise in mathematical optimization. Here, the mathematical optimization technique can be something quite brutish like trying all f values from 0 to 1.0 by .01. The objective function can be one of the functions presented in Chapter 1 for finding the geometric mean HPR for a given value of f under different conditions. The parameter is that value for f being tried between 0 and 1.

The answer returned by the objective function, along with the parameters pumped into the objective function, gives us our coordinates at a certain point in $n + 1$ space. In the case of simply finding the optimal f for a single market system or a single scenario spectrum, n is 1, so we are getting coordinates in two-dimensional space. One of the coordinates is the f value sent to the objective function, and the other coordinate is the value returned by the objective function for the f value passed to it.

Since it is a little difficult for us to mentally picture any more than three dimensions, we will think in terms of a value of 2 for n (thus, we are dealing with the three-dimensional, i.e., $n + 1$, landscape). Since, for simplicity's sake, we are using a value of 2 for n, the objective function gives us the height or *altitude* in a three-dimensional landscape. We can think of the north-south coordinates as corresponding to the f value associated with one scenario spectrum, and the east-west coordinates as the f value associated with another scenario spectrum. Each scenario spectrum pertains to the possible outcomes for a given market system. Thus, we could say, for example, that the north-south coordinates pertain to the f value for such-and-such a market under such and such a system, and the east-west coordinates pertain to the f values of trading either a different market and/or a different system, when both market systems are traded simultaneously.

The objective function gives us the altitude for a given set of f values. That is, the objective function gives us the altitude corresponding to a single east-west coordinate and a single north-south coordinate. That is, a single point where the length and depth are given by the f values we are pumping into the objective function, and the height at that point is the value returned by the objective function.

Once we have the coordinates for a single point (its length, depth, and height), we need a search procedure, a mathematical optimization technique, to alter the f values being pumped into the objective function in such a way so as to get us to the peak of the landscape as quickly and easily as possible.

What we are doing is trying to map out the terrain in the $n + 1$ dimensional landscape, because the coordinates corresponding to the peak in that landscape give us the optimal f values to use for each market system.

Many mathematical optimization techniques have been worked out over the years and many are quite elaborate and efficient. We have a number of these techniques to choose from. The burning question for us is, "Upon what objective function shall we apply these mathematical optimization techniques?" under this new framework. The objective function is the heart of this new framework in asset allocation, and we will discuss it and show examples of how to use it before looking at optimization techniques.

THE OBJECTIVE FUNCTION

The objective function we wish to maximize is the geometric mean HPR, simply called G:

$$G(f_1 \dots f_n) = \left(\prod_{k=1}^{m} \mathrm{HPR}_k \right)^{\left(1 / \sum_{k=1}^{m} \mathrm{Prob}_k \right)} \qquad [4.01]$$

where n = number of scenario spectrums (market systems or portfolio components).

        m = possible number of combinations of outcomes between the various scenario spectrums (market systems) based on how many scenarios are in each set. m = the number of scenarios in the first spectrum * the number of scenarios in the second spectrum *...* the number of scenarios in the nth spectrum.

      Prob = sum of probabilities of all m of the HPRs for a given set of f values. Prob_k is the sum of the values in brackets {} in Equation [4.02] for all m values of a given set of f values.

      HPR = The holding period return of each k. This is given as:

$$\mathrm{HPR}_k = \left(1 + \left(\sum_{i=1}^{n} (f_i * (-\mathrm{PL}_{k,i}/\mathrm{BL}_i)) \right) \right) \left\{ \left(\prod_{i=1}^{n-1} \left(\prod_{j=i+1}^{n} P(i_k \mid j_k) \right) \right)^{(1/(n-1))} \right\} \qquad [4.02]$$

where n = number of components (scenario spectrums, i.e., market systems) in the portfolio.

f_i = f value being used for component i. f_i must be >0, and can be infinitely high (i.e., can be greater than 1.0).

$PL_{k,i}$ = outcome profit or loss for the ith component (i.e., scenario spectrum or market system) associated with the kth combination of scenarios.

BL_i = worst outcome of scenario spectrum (market system) i.

Thus, $Prob_k$ in the earlier equation for G is:

$$Prob_k = \left(\prod_{i=1}^{n-1} \left(\prod_{j=i+1}^{n} P(i_k | j_k) \right) \right)^{(1/(n-1))}$$ [4.03]

The expression $P(i_k | j_k)$ is simply the joint probability (the subject of the last chapter) of the scenario in the ith spectrum and the jth spectrum, corresponding to the kth combination of scenarios. For example, if we have three coins, each coin represents a scenario spectrum, represented by the variable n, and each spectrum contains two scenarios: heads and tails. Thus, there are eight (2 * 2 * 2) possible combinations, represented by the variable m.

In Equation [4.01], the variable k proceeds from 1 to m, in *odometric* fashion:

Coin 1	Coin 2	Coin 3	k
t	t	t	1
t	t	h	2
t	h	t	3
t	h	h	4
h	t	t	5
h	t	h	6
h	h	t	7
h	h	h	8

That is, initially all spectrums are set to their worst (left-most) values. Then, the right-most scenario spectrum cycles through all of its values, after which the second right-most scenario spectrum increments to the next (next right) scenario. You proceed as such again, with the right-most scenario spectrum cycling through all of its scenarios, and when the second right-most scenario spectrum has cycled through all of its values, the third right-most scenario spectrum increments to its next scenario. The process is exactly the same as an odometer on a car, hence the term *odometrically.*

So in the expression $P(i_k|j_k)$, if k were at the value 3 above (i.e., $k = 3$), and i was 1 and j was 3, we would be looking for the joint probability of coin 1 coming up tails and coin 3 coming up tails. Finally, by substituting Equations [4.02] and [4.03] into [4.01], we can create one complete objective function. Thus, we wish to maximize G as:

$$G(f_i...f_n) = \left(\prod_{k=1}^{m} \left(\left(1 + \sum_{i=1}^{n} \left(f_i * \left(\frac{-PL_{k,i}}{BL_i} \right) \right) \right) \left(\left(\prod_{i=1}^{n-1} \left(\prod_{j=i+1}^{n} P(i_k|j_k) \right) \right)^{(1/(n-1))} \right) \right) \right) \left(1 / \sum_{k=1}^{m} \left(\left(\prod_{i=1}^{n-1} \left(\prod_{j=i+1}^{n} P(i_k|j_k) \right) \right)^{(1/(n-1))} \right) \right)$$

[4.04]

This is the objective function, the equation we wish to maximize. It is the equation or mathematical expression of this new framework in asset allocation. It gives you the *altitude,* the geometric mean HPR, in $n + 1$ space for the coordinates, the values of f used. It is *exact,* regardless of how many scenarios or scenario spectrums are used as input. *It is the objective function of the leverage space model.*

Although Equation [4.04] may look a little daunting, there isn't any reason to fear it. As you can see, Equation [4.04] is a lot easier to work with in the compressed form, expressed earlier in Equation [4.01].

Returning to our three coin example, suppose we win two dollars on heads and lose one dollar on tails. We have three scenario spectrums, three market systems, named Coin 1, Coin 2, and Coin 3. Two scenarios, heads and tails, comprise each coin, each scenario spectrum. We will assume, for the sake of simplicity, that the correlation coefficients of all three scenario spectrums (coins) to each other are 0.

We must therefore find three different f values. We are seeking an optimal f value for Coin 1, Coin 2, and Coin 3, as f_1, f_2, and f_3, respectively, that results in the greatest growth—that is, the combination of the three f values that results in the greatest geometric mean HPR (Equations [4.01] or [4.04]).

For the moment, we are not paying any attention to the optimization technique selected. The purpose here is to show how to perform the objective function. Since optimization techniques usually assign an initial value to the parameters, we will arbitrarily select .1 as the initial value for all three values of f.

We will use Equation [4.01] in lieu of [4.04] for the sake of simplicity. Equation [4.01] has us begin by cycling through all scenario set combinations, all values of k between 1 and m, compute the HPR of the scenario set combination per Equation [4.02], and multiply all of these HPRs together. When we perform Equation [4.02] each time, we must keep track of the exponents in brackets { }, because we will need the sum of these exponents later.

Thus we start at $k = 1$, where scenario spectrum 1 (Coin 1) is tails, as are the other two scenario spectrums (coins).

We can rewrite Equation [4.02] as:

$$\text{HPR}_k = (1 + C)^x$$

$$C = \sum_{i=1}^{n} (f_i * (-\text{PL}_{k,i}/\text{BL}_i)) \qquad [4.05]$$

$$x = \left(\prod_{i=1}^{n-1} \left(\prod_{j=i+1}^{n} P(i_k | j_k) \right) \right)^{(1/(n-1))}$$

Notice that the exponent in Equation [4.02] in brackets, which we must keep track of, is expressed as the variable x in Equation [4.05]. This is also expressed in Equation [4.03].

So, to obtain C, we simply go through each scenario spectrum, taking the outcome of the scenario currently being used in that spectrum as dictated by k, dividing its negative by the scenario in that spectrum with the worst outcome, and multiplying this quotient by the f value being used with that scenario spectrum. As we go through all of the scenario spectrums, we total these values.

The variable i is the scenario spectrum we are looking at. The biggest loss in scenario spectrum 1 is tails, which sees a loss of one dollar (i.e., -1). Thus, BL_1 is -1 (as will be BL_2 and BL_3 since the biggest loss in each of the other two scenario spectrums—the other two coins—is -1). The associated PL, that is, the outcome of the scenario in spectrum i corresponding to the scenario in that spectrum that k points to, is -1 in scenario spectrum 1 (as it is in the other two spectrums). The f value is currently .1 (as it also is now in the other two spectrums). Thus:

$$C = \sum_{i=1}^{n} \left(f_i * \left(\frac{-\text{PL}_{k,i}}{\text{BL}_i} \right) \right)$$

$$C = \left(.1 * \left(\frac{--1}{-1} \right) \right) + \left(.1 * \left(\frac{--1}{-1} \right) \right) + \left(-1 * \left(\frac{--1}{-1} \right) \right)$$

$$C = (.1 * -1) + (.1 * -1) + (.1 * -1)$$

$$C = -.1 + -.1 + -.1 = -.3$$

Notice that the PLs are negative and, since PL has a minus sign in front of it, that makes them positive.

Now we take the value for C in Equation [4.05] and add 1 to it, obtaining .7 (since $1 + -3 = .7$). Now we must figure the exponent, the variable x in Equation [4.05].

$P(i_k | j_k)$ means, simply, the joint probability of the scenario in spectrum i pointed to by k, and the scenario in spectrum j pointed to by k. Since k is presently 1, it points to tails in all three scenario spectrums. To find x, we simply take the sum of the joint probabilities of the scenarios in spectrum 1 and 2 times the joint probability of the scenarios in spectrum 1 and 3, times the joint probabilities of the scenarios in spectrums 2 and 3. Expressed differently:

i	j
1	2
1	3
2	3

If there were four spectrums, we would take the product of all the joint probabilities as:

i	j
1	2
1	3
1	4
2	3
2	4
3	4

Since all of our joint probabilities are .25, we get for x:

$$x = \left(\prod_{i=1}^{n-1} \left(\prod_{j=i+1}^{n} P(i_k | j_k) \right) \right)^{(1/(n-1))}$$

$$x = (.25 * .25)^{(1/(n-1))}$$

$$x = (.015625)^{1/(3-1)}$$

$$x = (.015625)^{1/2}$$

$$x = .125$$

Thus, x equals .125, which represents the joint probability of the kth combination of scenarios. (Note that we are going to determine a joint probability of three random variables by using joint probabilities of two random variables!)

Thus, $HPR_k = .7^{.125} = .9563949076$ when $k = 1$. Per Equation [4.02] or [4.05], we must figure this for all values of k from 1 through m (in this case, m equals 8). Doing this, we obtain:

k	HPR_k	$Prob_k$
1	0.956395	0.125
2	1	0.125
3	1	0.125
4	1.033339	0.125
5	1	0.125
6	1.033339	0.125
7	1.033339	0.125
8	1.060511	0.125

Summing up all the $Prob_k$, given by Equation [4.03], per Equation [4.04], we get 1. Now, taking the product of all of the HPRs, per Equations [4.01] and [4.04], we obtain 1.119131. Performing Equation [4.01] then, we get a value of G of 1.119131 which corresponds to the f values .1, .1, .1 for $f_1, f_2,$ and f_3, respectively.

$$G(.1,.1,.1) = \left(\prod_{k=1}^{m} HPR_k \right)^{\left(1 / \sum_{k=1}^{m} Prob_k \right)}$$

$$G(.1,.1,.1) = (.956395 * 1 * .1 * 1.033339 * 1 * 1.033339$$
$$* 1.033339 * 1.0605011)^{(1/(.125 + .125 + .125 + .125 + .125 + .125 + .125 + .125))}$$

$$G(.1,.1,.1) = (1.119131)^{(1/1)}$$

$$G(.1,.1,.1) = 1.119131$$

Now, depending upon what mathematical optimization method we were using, we would alter our f values. Eventually, we would find our optimal f values at .21, .21, .21 for $f_1, f_2,$ and f_3, respectively. This would give us:

k	HPR_k	$Prob_k$
1	0.883131	0.125
2	1	0.125
3	1	0.125
4	1.062976	0.125
5	1	0.125
6	1.062976	0.125
7	1.062976	0.125
8	1.107296	0.125

Thus, Equation [4.01] gives us:

$$G(.21,.21,.21) = \left(\prod_{k=1}^{m} HPR_k\right)^{\left(1/\sum_{k=1}^{m} Prob_k\right)}$$

$$G(.21,.21,.21) = (.883131 * 1 * .1 * 1.062976 * 1 * 1.062976$$
$$* 1.062976 * 1.107296)^{(1/(.125 + .125 + .125 + .125 + .125 + .125 + .125 + .125))}$$

$$G(.21,.21,.21) = 1.174516^{(1/1)}$$

$$G(.21,.21,.21) = 1.174516$$

This is the f value combination that results in the greatest G for these scenario spectrums. Since this is a very simplified case, i.e., all scenario spectrums were identical, and all had correlation of 0 between them, we ended up with the same f value for all three scenario spectrums of .21. Usually, this will not be the case, and you will have a different f value for each scenario spectrum.

Now that we know the optimal f values for each scenario spectrum, we can determine how much those decimal f values are, in currency, by dividing the largest loss scenario in each of the spectrums by the negative optimal f for each of those spectrums. For example, for the first scenario spectrum, Coin 1, we had a largest loss of -1. Dividing -1 by the negative optimal f, $-.21$, we obtain 4.761904762 as $f\$$ for Coin 1.

To summarize the procedure then:

1. Start with an f value set for $f_1 \ldots f_n$ where n is the number of components in the portfolio, i.e., market systems or scenario spectrums. This initial f value set is given by the optimization technique selected.

2. Go through the combinations of scenario sets k from 1 to m, odometrically, and calculate an HPR for each k, multiplying them all together. While doing so, keep a running sum of the exponents of the HPRs.

3. When k equals m, and you have computed the last HPR, the final product must be taken to the power of 1, divided by the sum of the exponents (probabilities) of all the HPRs, to get G, the geometric mean HPR.

4. This geometric mean HPR gives us one *altitude* in $n + 1$ space. We wish to find the peak in this space, so we must now select a new set of f values to test to help us find the peak. This is the mathematical optimization process.

MATHEMATICAL OPTIMIZATION VS. ROOT FINDING

Equations have a left and a right side. Subtracting the two makes the equation equal to 0. In *root finding,* you want to know what values of the independent variable(s) make the answer of this equation equal to 0 (these are the *roots*). There are traditional root-finding techniques, such as the *Newton-Rapheson* method, to do this.

It would seem that root finding is related to mathematical optimization in that the first derivative of an optimized function (i.e., extremum located) will equal 0. Thus, you would assume that traditional root-finding techniques, such as the Newton-Rapheson method, could be used to solve optimization problems (however, to use what is regarded as an optimization technique to solve for the roots of an equation can lead to a Pandora's box of problems).

However, our discussion will concern only optimization techniques and not root finding techniques per se. The single best source for a listing of these techniques is *Numerical Recipes.*[1]

OPTIMIZATION TECHNIQUES

Mathematical optimization, in short, can be described as follows: You have a function (we call it G), the objective function, which depends on one or more independent variables (which we call $f_1 \ldots f_n$). You want to find the value(s) of the independent variable(s) which results in a minimum (or sometimes, as in our case, a maximum) of the objective function. Maximization or minimization is essentially the same thing (that is one person's G is another person's $-G$).

In the crudest case, you can optimize as follows: take every combination of parameters, run them through the objective function, and see which produce the best results. For example, suppose we want to find the optimal f for two coins tossed simultaneously, and we want the answer to be precise to .01. We could, therefore, test Coin 1 at the 0.0 level, while testing Coin 2 at the 0.01 level, then .01, .02, and proceed until we have tested Coin 2 at the 1.0 level. Then, we could go back and test with Coin 1 at the .01 level, and cycle Coin 2 through all of its possible values while holding Coin 1 at the .01 level. We proceed until both levels are at their maximum, i.e., both values equal 1.0. Since each variable in this case has 101 possible values (0 through 1.0 by .01 inclusive), there are 101 * 101 combinations which must be tried, or, 10,201 times the objective function must be evaluated.

We could, if we wanted, demand precision greater than .01. Suppose we wanted precision to the .001 level. Then we would have 1,001 * 1,001 combinations which we would need to try, or 1,002,001 times the objective function would have to be calculated. If we were then to include three variables rather than just two, and demand .001 precision this way, we would then have to evaluate the objective function 1001 * 1001 * 1001, or 1,003,003,001; that is, we would have to evaluate the objective function in excess of one billion times. We are using only three variables and we are demanding precision to only .001!

Although this crude case of optimizing has the advantage of being the most robust of all optimization techniques, it is also has the dubious distinction of being too slow to apply to most problems.

Why not cycle through all variables for the first variable and get its optimal; then cycle through all variables for the second while holding the first at its optimal; get the second variable's optimal, so that you now have the optimal for the first two parameters; Go find the optimal for the third while setting the first two to their optimal, etc., until you have solved the problem?

The problem with this second approach is that it is often impossible to find the optimum parameter set this way. Notice that by the time we get to the third variable, the first two variables equal their optimum as if there were no other variables. Thus, when the third variable is optimized, with the first two variables set to their optimums, they interfere with the solution of the third optimum. What you would end up with is not the optimum parameter set of the three variables, but, rather, an optimum value for the first parameter, an optimum for the second when the first is set to its optimum, an optimum for the third when the first is set to its optimum, and the second set to a suboptimum, but optimum given the interference of the first, etc. It may be possible to keep cycling through the variables and eventually resolve to the optimum parameter set, but with more than three variables, it becomes more and more lengthy, if at all possible, given the interference of the other variables.

There exists superior techniques which have been devised, rather than the two crude methods described, for mathematical optimization. This is a fascinating branch of modern mathematics, and I strongly urge you to study it, simply in the hope that you derive a fraction of the satisfaction from the study as I have.

An extremum, that is the maximum or minimum, can be either *global* (truly the highest or lowest value) or *local* (the highest or lowest value in the immediate neighborhood). To truly know a global extremum is nearly impossible, since you do not know the range of values of the independent variables. If you do know the range, then you have simply found a local extremum. Therefore, oftentimes, when people speak of a global extremum, they are really referring to a local extremum over a very wide range of values for the independent variables.

There are a number of techniques for finding the maximum or minimum in such cases. Usually, in any type of mathematical optimization, there are *constraints* placed on the variables which must be met with respect to the extremum. For example, in our case, there are the constraints that all independent variables (the f values) must be greater than or equal to 0. Oftentimes, there are constraining functions which must be met [i.e., other functions involving the variable(s) used which must be above/below or equal to certain values]. *Linear programming,* including the *simplex algorithm,* is one very well developed area of this type of constrained optimization, but will only work where the function to be optimized and the constraint functions are linear functions (first-degree polynomials).

Generally, the different methods for mathematical optimization can be broken down by the following categories, and the appropriate technique selected:

1. Single variable (two-dimensional) vs. multivariable (three- or more dimensional) objective functions.
2. Linear methods vs. nonlinear methods. That is, as previously mentioned, if the function to be optimized and the constraint functions are linear functions (i.e., do not have exponents greater than 1 to any of the terms in the functions), there are a number of very well developed techniques for solving for extrema.
3. Derivatives. Some methods require computation of the first derivative of the objective function. In the multivariable case, the first derivative is a vector quantity called the *gradient.*
4. Computational efficiency. That is, you want to find the extremum as quickly (i.e., with as few computations) and easily (something to consider with those techniques which require calculation of the derivative) as possible, using as little computer storage as possible.
5. Robustness. Remember, you want to find the extremum which is local to a very wide range of parameter values, to act as a surrogate global extremum. Therefore, if there is more than one extremum in this range, you do not want to get hung up on the less extreme extremum.

In our discussion, we are concerned only with the multidimensional case. That is, we concern ourselves only with those optimization algorithms that pertain to two or more variables (i.e., more than one scenario set). **In searching for a single f value, that is, in finding the f of one market system or one scenario set,** *parabolic interpolation,* **as detailed in** *Portfolio Management Formulas,* **will generally be the quickest and most efficient technique.**

In the multidimensional case, there are many good algorithms, yet there is no perfect algorithm. Some methods work better than others for certain types of problems. Generally, personal preference is the main determinant in selecting a multidimensional optimization technique (provided one has the computer hardware necessary for the chosen technique).

Multidimensional techniques can be classified according to five broad categories.

First, are the *hill climbing simplex methods*. These are perhaps the least efficient of all, if the computational burden gets a little heavy. However, they are often easy to implement and do not require the calculation of partial first derivatives. Unfortunately, they tend to be slow and their storage requirements are on the order of n^2.

The second family are the *direction set methods,* also known as the *line minimization methods* or *conjugate direction methods*. Most notable among these are the various methods of Powell. These are more efficient, in terms of speed, than the hill climbing simplex methods (not to be confused with the simplex algorithm for linear functions mentioned earlier), do not require the calculation of partial first derivatives, yet the storage requirements are still on the order of n^2.

The third family is the *conjugate gradient methods*. Notable among these are the Fletcher–Reeves method and the closely related Polak–Ribiere method. These tend to be among the most efficient of all methods in terms of speed and storage (requiring storage on the order of n times x), yet they do require calculations of partial first derivatives.

The fourth family of multidimensional optimization techniques are the *quasi-Newton,* or *variable metric methods*. These include the Davidson–Fletcher–Powell (DFP) and the Broyden–Fletcher–Goldfarb–Shanno (BFGS) algorithms. Like the conjugate gradient methods, these require calculation of partial first derivatives, tend to rapidly converge to an extremum, yet these require greater storage, on the order of n^2. However, the tradeoff to the conjugate gradient methods is that these have been around longer, are in more widespread use, and have greater documentation.

The fifth family is the *natural simulation* family of multidimensional optimization techniques. These are by far the most fascinating, as they seek extrema by simulating processes found in nature, where nature herself is thought to seek extrema. Among these techniques are the *genetic algorithm* method, which seeks extrema through a survival-of-the-fittest process, and *simulated annealing,* a technique which simulates crystallization, a process whereby a system finds its minimum energy state. These techniques tend to be the most robust of all methods, nearly immune to local extrema, and can solve problems of gigantic complexity. However, they are not necessarily the quickest, and, in most cases, will not be. These techniques are still so new that very little is known about them yet.

Although you can use any of the aforementioned multidimensional optimization algorithms, I have opted for the genetic algorithm because it is perhaps the single most robust mathematical optimization technique, aside from the very crude technique of attempting every variable combination.

It is a *general* optimization and search method that has been applied to many problems. Often it is used in neural networks, since it has the characteristic of scaling well to noisy or large nonlinear problems. Since the technique does not require gradient information, it can also be applied to discontinuous functions, as well as empirical functions, just as it is applied to analytic functions.

The algorithm, although frequently used in neural networks, is not limited solely to them. Here, we can use it as a technique for finding the optimal point in the $n + 1$ dimensional landscape.

SURVIVAL OF THE FITTEST

The genetic algorithm is supposed to replicate the survival-of-the-fittest principle in nature. This it does, but not exactly as nature does. In fact, we really don't know a great deal about how nature invokes this principle.

First of all, in the natural world, if you take a population of identical candidates, one will always emerge the winner; i.e., it will be regarded as the most fit. This is true even if all the candidates are the same!

For example, if I throw a bunch of coins on the table, and use another coin as the "flipping" coin, I can play the following game. The coins on the table are evenly divided, either heads or tails. I flip the flipping coin and, if it is heads, I remove a coin that is heads. If it is tails, I remove a coin that is tails. The game is over when there are only all heads or all tails remaining.

It is a stupid game, but it proves the point that being neither heads nor tails has a selective advantage in this game (both have equal probabilities of being the winner), yet one will emerge the winner, i.e., be *the fittest.*

So when we ask, "Which candidate is the most fit?", we are met with the paradoxical answer, "The one who is the winner."

Also, it appears that nature has many different objective functions. If it didn't, the world would eventually have become inhabited by amphibians who could fly—fast! For instance, how can you explain the existence of something such as the hummingbird? It has a terrible, immediate dependency on sugars, is not intelligent in comparison to humans, yet survives along with so many other species on the planet. Clearly, the hummingbird has found a niche in the natural order of the planet—an objective function offered by nature which the hummingbird satisfies to the extent that it has not become extinct.

The genetic algorithm, by contrast, is much simpler. Here, we have one objective function we are trying to satisfy. So, although we say that the genetic algorithm is modeled after a natural process, it is so much simpler than the natural process that it hardly deserves its name.

THE GENETIC ALGORITHM

In a nutshell, the algorithm works by examining many possible candidate solutions and ranking them on how well their value output, by whatever objective function, is used. Then, like the theory of natural selection, the most fit survive and reproduce a new generation of candidate solutions, which inherit characteristics of both *parent* solutions of the earlier generation. The average fitness of the population will increase over many generations and approach an optimum.

The main drawback to the algorithm is the large amount of processing overhead required to evaluate and maintain the candidate solutions. However, due to its robust nature and effective implementation to the gamut of optimization problems, however large, nonlinear, or noisy, it is this author's contention that it will become the de facto optimization technique of choice in the future (excepting the emergence of a better algorithm which possesses these desirable characteristics). As computers become ever more powerful and inexpensive, the processing overhead required of the genetic algorithm becomes less of a concern. Truly, if processing speed was zero, if speed was not a factor, the genetic algorithm would be the optimization method of choice for nearly all mathematical optimization problems.

The basic steps involved in the algorithm are as follows:

1. *Gene length.* You must determine the length of a *gene*. A gene is the binary representation of one member of the population of candidate solutions, and each member of this population carries a value for each variable (i.e., an *f* value for each scenario spectrum). Thus, if we allow a gene length of twelve times the number of scenario spectrums, we have twelve bits assigned to each variable (i.e., *f* value). Twelve bits allows for values in the range of 0 to 4095. This is figured as:

$$2^0 + 2^1 + 2^2 + ... + 2^{11} = 4095$$

Simply take 2 to the 0th power plus 2 to the next power, until you reach the power of the number of bits minus 1 (i.e., 11 in this case). If there are, say, three scenario spectrums, and we are using a length of twelve bits per scenario spectrum, then the length of a gene for each candidate solution is $12 * 3 = 36$ bits. That is, the gene in this case is a string of thirty-six bits of 1s and 0s.

Notice that this method of encoding the bit strings only allows for integer values. We can have it allow for floating-point values as well by using a uniform divisor. Thus, if we select a uniform divisor of say, 1,000, then we can store values of 0/1000 to 4095/1000, or 0 to 4.095, and get precision down to .001.

What we need then is a routine to convert the candidate solutions to encoded binary strings and back again.

2. *Initialization.* A starting population is required—that is, a population of candidate solutions. The bit strings of this first generation are encoded randomly. Larger population sizes make it more likely that we will find a good solution, but they require more processing time.

3. *Objective function evaluation.* The bit strings are decoded to their decimal equivalents, and are used to evaluate the objective function. (The objective function, for example, if we are looking at two scenario spectrums, gives us the *Z* coordinate value, the altitude of the three-dimensional terrain, assuming the *f* values of the respective scenario spectrums are the *X* and *Y* coordinates.) This is performed for all candidate solutions, and their objective functions are saved. (*Important:* Objective function values must be nonnegative!)

4. *Reproduction*
    a. *Scaling based upon fitness.* The objective functions are now scaled. This is accomplished by first determining the lowest

objective function of all the candidate solutions, and subtracting this value from all candidate solutions. The results of this are summed up. Then, each objective function has the smallest objective function subtracted from it, and the result is divided by the sum of these, to obtain a fitness score between 0 and 1. The sums of the fitness scores of all candidate solutions will then be 1.0.

b. *Random selection based upon fitness.* The scaled objective functions are now aligned as follows. If, say, the first objective function has a scaled fitness score of .05, the second has one of .1, and the third .08, then they are set up in a selection scheme as follows:

first candidate	0 to .05
second candidate	.05 to .15
third candidate	.15 to .23

This continues until the last candidate has its upper limit at 1.0.

Now, two random numbers are generated between 0 and 1, with the random numbers determining from the preceding selection scheme who the two parents will be. Two parents must now be selected for each candidate solution of the next generation.

c. *Crossover.* Go through each bit of the *child,* the new population candidate. Start by copying the first bit of the first parent to the first bit of the child. At each bit carryover, you must also generate a random number. If the random number is less than or equal to (probability of crossover/gene length), then switch to copying the bits over from the other parent. Thus, if we have three scenario spectrums and twelve bits per each variable, then the gene length is thirty-six. If we use a probability of crossover of .6, then the random number generated at any bit must be less than .6/36, or less than .01667, in order to switch to copying the other parent's code for subsequent bits. Continue until all the bits are copied to the child. This must be performed for all new population candidates.

Typically, probabilities of crossover are in the range .6 to .9. Thus, a .9 probability of crossover means there is a 90%

chance, on average, that there will be crossover to the child; i.e., a 10% chance the child will be an exact replicant of one of the parents.

d.   *Mutation.*   While copying over each bit from parent to child, generate a second random number. If this random number is less than or equal to the probability of mutation, then toggle that bit. Thus, a bit which is 0 in the parent becomes 1 in the child and vice versa. Mutation helps maintain diversity in the population. The probability of mutation should generally be some small value (i.e., <=.001); otherwise the algorithm tends to deteriorate into a random search. As the algorithm approaches an optimum, however, mutation becomes more and more important, since crossover cannot maintain genetic diversity in such a localized space in the $n + 1$ terrain.

Now you can go back to step three and perform the process for the next generation. Along the way, you must keep track of the highest objective function returned and its corresponding gene. Keep repeating the process until you have reached X unimproved generations, that is, X generations where the best objective function value has not been exceeded. You then quit, at that point, and use the gene corresponding to that best objective function value as your solution set.

For an example of implementing the genetic algorithm, suppose our objective function is one of the form:

$$Y = 1500 - (X - 15)^2$$

For the sake of simplicity in illustration, we will have only a single variable; thus, each population member only carries the binary code for that one variable.

Upon inspection, we can see that the optimal value for X is 15, which would result in a Y value of 1500. However, rarely will we know what the optimal values for the variables are, but for the sake of this simple illustration, it will help if we know the optimal so that we can see how the algorithm takes us there.

Assume a starting population of three members, each with the variable values encoded in five-bit strings, and each initially random:

First Generation

Individual #	X	Binary X	Y	Fitness Score
1	10	01010	1475	.4751
2	0	00000	1275	0
3	13	01101	1496	.5249

Now, through random selection based on fitness, Individual number 1 for the second generation draws Parents 1 and 3 from the first generation (note that Parent 2, with a fitness of 0, has died and will not pass on its genetic characteristics). Assume that random crossover occurs after the fourth bit, so that Individual 1 in the second generation inherits the first four bits from Individual 1 of the first generation, and the last bit from Individual 3 of the first generation, producing 01011 for Individual 1 of the second generation.

Assume Individual 2 for the second generation also draws the same parents; crossover occurs only after the first and third bits. Thus, it inherits bit 0 from Individual 1 in the first generation, bit 11 as the second and third bits from the third individual in the first generation, and the last two bits from the first individual of the first generation, producing 01110 as the genetic code for the second individual in the second generation.

Now, assume that the third individual of the second generation draws Individual 1 as its first parent as well as its second. Thus, the third individual in the second generation ends up with exactly the same genetic material as the first individual in the first generation, or 01010.

Second Generation

Individual #	X	Binary X
1	11	01011
2	14	01110
3	10	01010

Now, through random mutation, the third bit of the first individual is flipped, and the resulting values are used to evaluate the objective function:

	Second Generation			
Individual #	X	Binary X	Y	Fitness Score
1	15	01111	1500	.5102
2	14	01110	1499	.4898
3	10	01010	1475	0

Notice how the average Y score has gone up, or evolved, after two generations.

IMPORTANT NOTES

It is often advantageous to carry the strongest individual's code to the next generation in its entirety. By so doing, good solution sets are certain to be maintained, and this has the effect of expediting the algorithm. Then, you can work to aggressively maintain genetic diversity by increasing the values used for the probability of crossover and the probability of mutation. I have found that you can work with a probability of crossover of 2, a probability of mutation of .05, and converge to solutions quicker, provided you retain the code of the most fit individual from one generation to the next, which keeps the algorithm from deteriorating to a random search.

As population size approaches infinity, that is, as you use a larger and larger value for the population size, the answer converged upon is exact. Likewise, with the unimproved generations parameter, as it approaches infinity—that is, as you use a larger and larger value for unimproved generations—the answer converged upon is exact. However, both of these parameter increases are at the expense of extra computing time.

The algorithm can be time intensive. As the number of scenario sets increases, and the number of scenarios increases, the processing time grows geometrically. Depending upon your time constraints, you may wish to keep your scenario sets and the quantity of scenarios to a manageable number. Computer speed (that is, access to the fastest computer you can get) is very beneficial here.

Once you have found the optimal portfolio, that is, once you have f values, you simply divide those f values by the largest loss scenario of the respective scenario spectrums to determine the $f\$$ for that particular scenario spectrum. This is exactly as we did in the first chapter for determining how many contracts to trade in an optimal portfolio.

REFERENCE

1. William H. Press, Brian P. Flannery, Saul A. Teukolsky, and William T. Vetterling, *Numerical Recipes: The Art of Scientific Computing,* New York: Cambridge University Press, 1986.

5

Money Management for Money Managers

Asset Allocation is the primary exercise for money managers. A recent study[1] done by Brinson, Singer, and Beebower of 82 large pension plans over a ten-year period found that a plan's asset allocation policy explained 91.5% of the return earned. Active investment decisions by plan sponsors and managers pertaining to both selection and timing, contributed very little to performance, whereas the asset allocation policy was the overwhelmingly dominant contributor.

Why is it that so many investment programs are characterized by an asset allocation policy which is arbitrary instead of one which is mathematically based? We are, no doubt, surrounded by ignorance. Further, with the proliferation of derivatives trading and leveraged instruments, the asset allocation puzzle gets cloudier still, and the tendency for arbitrary allocation grows. Investment managers need a new framework for analyzing their asset allocation policies that is mathematically based and takes leverage, with both its meanings, into account.

We can find the peak of the n + 1 dimensional landscape of leverage space via the new model presented in the previous chapter. Unfortunately, money managers must live within a given set of constraints that, in most cases, would prohibit them from residing at the peak in this landscape. The drawdowns will almost always be more than what their investors will allow. However, this inability to be at the peak does not mean that they cannot use the new framework to make beneficial choices.

Thus, this chapter attempts to seek viable alternatives, in the context of this new framework, to being at the peak in the n + 1 dimensional landscape. Instead, this new framework offers us other beneficial ways of navigating through it. Since, ultimately, all investment managers reside somewhere on the landscape, they should realize that it can be beneficial to operate within the framework in some other fashion than what they are doing, even if they cannot afford the drawdowns of being at the peak of the landscape. These other beneficial alternatives are the subject of this chapter, along with many of the real-life obstacles, such as margin requirements, with which money managers are faced in implementing this new framework.

IMPLEMENTING THE NEW MODEL

Usually, as you enter into a holding period, you will know which markets and systems (i.e., scenario spectrums) you will be investing in, as well as which ones have positions already established from prior holding periods which you are carrying into the new holding period. Furthermore, you will, more than likely, be altering the scenarios within the various scenario spectrums to reflect more current information (either their probabilities, outcomes, both), or creating and deleting new scenarios within the various scenario spectrums.

These aspects do not present a problem. What must be done is that the optimal portfolio must be determined for all positions which you are carrying into the new holding period, based on the new information. These positions must be adjusted to reflect the quantities suggested by the model so that you are always carrying what is regarded as the optimal allocations. Whenever you are about to enter into a new position, you should once again determine the optimal portfolio per the new model, and once again alter your positions so that you are carrying positions in what is currently regarded as the optimal allocations.

In short, always rerun the model coming into each new holding period to reflect any changes made to the input information, and always carry what is presently shown as optimal.

ACTIVE AND INACTIVE EQUITY

If we are trading a portfolio at the full optimal allocations, we can expect tremendous drawdowns on the entire portfolio in terms of equity retracement. Our only guard against this is to dilute the portfolio somewhat. The degree of risk and safety to any investment, therefore, is not a function of the investment itself, but rather a function of the level of dilution.

Even a portfolio of blue chip stocks, if traded at their geometric optimal portfolio levels, will show tremendous drawdowns. Yet, these blue chip stocks must be traded at these levels, as these levels maximize potential geometric gain relative to dispersion (risk), and also provide for attaining a goal in the least possible time. When viewed from such a perspective, trading blue chip stocks is no more risky than trading pork bellies, and pork bellies are no less conservative than blue chip stocks. The same can be said of a portfolio of commodity trading systems and a portfolio of bonds.

Typically, investors practice dilution, whether inadvertent or not. That is, if, optimally, one should trade a certain component in a portfolio at the $f\$$ level of, say, \$2,500, they may be trading it consciously at an $f\$$ level of, say, \$5,000, in a conscious effort to smooth out the equity curve and buffer drawdowns, or, unconsciously, at such a half-optimal f level, since all positions can be assigned an f value as detailed in Chapter 1.

Another way you can practice asset allocation is by splitting your equity into two subaccounts, an active subaccount and an inactive subaccount. These are not two separate accounts; rather, in theory, they are a way of splitting a single account.

The technique works as follows. First, you must decide upon an initial fractional level. Let's suppose that, initially, you want to. emulate an account at the half f level. Therefore, your initial fractional level is .5 (the initial fractional level must be greater than 0, and less than 1). This means you will split your account, with .5 of the equity in your account going into the inactive subaccount and .5 going into the active subaccount. Let's assume we are starting out with a \$100,000 account. Therefore, \$50,000 is initially in the inactive subaccount and \$50,000 is in the active subaccount. It is the equity in the active subaccount that you use to determine how many units to trade. These subaccounts are not real; they are a hypothetical construct you are creating in order to manage your money more effectively. You always use the full optimal fs with this technique. Any equity changes are reflected in the active portion of the account. Therefore, each day, you must look at the account's total equity (closed equity plus open equity, marking open positions to the market) and subtract the inactive amount (which will remain constant from day to day). The difference is your active equity, and it is on this difference that you will calculate how many units to trade at the full f levels.

Let's suppose that the optimal f for market system A is to trade one contract for every $2,500 in account equity. You come into the first day with $50,000 in active equity and, therefore, you will look to trade twenty units. If you were using the straight half f strategy, you would end up with the same number of units on day one. At half f, you would trade one contract for every $5,000 in account equity ($2,500/.5) and you would use the full $100,000 account equity to figure how many units to trade. Therefore, under the half f strategy, you would trade twenty units on this day as well.

However, as soon as the equity in the account changes, the number of units you will trade changes as well. Let's assume that you make $5,000 this next day, thus pushing the total equity in the account up to $105,000. Under the half f strategy, you will now be trading twenty-one units. However, under the split equity technique, you must subtract the now-constant inactive amount of $50,000 from your total equity of $105,000. This leaves an active equity portion of $55,000, from which you will figure your contract size at the optimal f level of one contract for every $2,500 in equity. Therefore, under the split equity technique, you will now look to trade twenty-two units.

The procedure works the same on the downside of the equity curve as well, with the split equity technique peeling off units at a faster rate than the fractional f strategy. Suppose we lost $5,000 on the first day of trading, putting the total account equity at $95,000. Under the fractional f strategy, you would now look to trade nineteen units ($95,000/$5,000). However, under the split equity technique you are now left with $45,000 of active equity and, thus, you will look to trade eighteen units ($45,000/$2,500).

Notice that with the split equity technique, the exact fraction of optimal f that we are using changes with the equity changes. We specify the fraction we want to start with. In our example, we used an initial fraction of .5. When the equity increases, this fraction of the optimal f increases, too, approaching 1 as a limit as the account equity approaches infinity. On the downside, this fraction approaches 0 as a limit at the level where the total equity in the account equals the inactive portion. This fact, that there is built-in portfolio insurance with the split equity technique, is a tremendous benefit and will be discussed at length later in this chapter.

Because the split equity technique has a fraction for f which moves, we will refer to it as a dynamic fractional f strategy, as opposed to the straight fractional f (which we will call a *static* fractional f) strategy.

Using the dynamic fractional f technique is analogous to trading an account full out at the optimal f levels, where the initial size of the account is the active equity portion.

So, we see that there are two ways to dilute an account down from the full geometric optimal portfolio. We can trade a static fractional or a dynamic fractional f. Although the two techniques are related, they also differ. Which is best?

To begin with, we need to be able to determine the arithmetic average HPR for trading n given scenario spectrums simultaneously, as well as the variance in those HPRs for those n simultaneously traded scenario spectrums, for given f values ($f_1...f_n$) operating on those scenario spectrums. These are given now as:

$\text{AHPR}(f_i...f_n) =$

$$\frac{\sum\limits_{k=1}^{m}\left[\left(1 + \sum\limits_{i=1}^{n}\left(f_i * \left(\frac{-\text{PL}_{k,i}}{\text{BL}_i}\right)\right)\right) * \left\{\left(\prod\limits_{i=1}^{n-1}\prod\limits_{j=i+1}^{n} P(i_a|j_a)\right)^{(1/(n-1))}\right\}\right]}{\sum\limits_{k=1}^{m}\text{Prob}_k} \qquad [5.01]$$

where n = number of scenario spectrums (market systems or portfolio components).

m = possible number of combinations of outcomes between the various scenario spectrums (market systems) based on how many scenarios are in each set. m = the number of scenarios in the first spectrum $*$ the number of scenarios in the second spectrum $* ... *$ the number of scenarios in the nth spectrum.

Prob = sum of probabilities of all m of the HPRs for a given set of f values. Prob_k is the sum of the values in brackets {} in the numerator, for all m values of a given set of f values.

f_i = f value being used for component i. f_i must be >0, and can be infinitely high (i.e., it can be greater than 1.0).

$PL_{k,i}$ = outcome profit or loss for the ith component (i.e., scenario spectrum or market system) associated with the kth combination of scenarios.

BL_i = worst outcome of scenario spectrum (market system) i.

Thus, $Prob_k$ in the equation is equal to Equation [4.03].

Equation [5.01] simply takes the coefficient of each HPR *times* its probability and sums these. The resultant sum is then divided by the sum of the probabilities.

The variance in the HPRs for a given set of multiple simultaneous scenario spectrums being traded at given f values can be determined by first taking the *raw coefficient* of the HPRs, the rawcoef:

$$\text{rawcoef}_k = 1 + \sum_{i=1}^{n} \left(f_i * \left(\frac{-PL_{k,i}}{BL_i} \right) \right) \qquad [5.02]$$

Then, these raw coefficients are averaged for all values of k between 1 and m, to obtain arimeanrawcoef:

$$\text{arimeanrawcoef} = \frac{\left(\sum_{k=1}^{m} \text{rawcoef}_k \right)}{m} \qquad [5.03]$$

Now, the variance V can be determined as:

$$V = \frac{\sum_{k=1}^{m} (\text{rawcoef}_k - \text{arimeanrawcoef})^2 * \text{Prob}_k}{\sum_{k=1}^{m} \text{Prob}_k} \qquad [5.04]$$

Where again, $Prob_k$ is determined by Equation [4.03].

Why do we need this stuff? If you'll recall the fundamental equation from Chapter 1, knowing the arithmetic average HPR and the variance in those HPRs can be quite useful, particularly as we shall now see.

If we know what the AHPR is, and the variance at a given f level (say the optimal f level for argument's sake), we can convert these numbers into what they would be trading at a level of dilution we'll call FRAC. And, since we are able to figure out the two legs of the right triangle, we can also figure the estimated geometric mean HPR at the diluted level. The formulas are now given for the diluted AHPR, called FAHPR, the diluted standard deviation (which is simply the square root of variance), called FSD, and the diluted geometric mean HPR, called FGHPR here:

$$FAHPR = (AHPR - 1) * FRAC + 1 \qquad [5.05]$$

$$FSD = SD * FRAC \qquad [5.06]$$

$$FGHPR = \sqrt{FAHPR^2 - FSD^2} \qquad [5.07]$$

where   FRAC = fraction of optimal f we are solving for
        AHPR = arithmetic average HPR at the optimal f
          SD = standard deviation in HPRs at the optimal f
    FAHPR = arithmetic average HPR at the fractional f
      FSD = standard deviation in HPRs at the fractional f
  FGHPR = geometric average HPR at the fractional f

Let's assume we have a system where the AHPR is 1.0265. The standard deviation in these HPRs is .1211 (i.e., this is the square root of the variance given by Equation [5.04]); therefore, the estimated geometric mean is 1.019. Now, we will look at the numbers for a .2 static fractional f and a .1 static fractional f. The results, then, are:

	Full f	.2 f	.1 f
AHPR	1.0265	1.0053	1.00265
SD	.1211	.02422	.01211
GHPR	1.01933	1.005	1.002577

Here is what will also prove to be a useful equation, the time expected to reach a specific goal:

$$T = \frac{\ln(\text{goal})}{\ln(\text{geometric mean})} \qquad [5.08a]$$

where T = expected number of holding periods to reach a specific
          goal
    goal = goal in terms of a multiple on our starting stake, a TWR
    ln( ) = natural logarithm function

Now, we will compare trading at the .2 static fractional f strategy, with a geometric mean of 1.005, to the .2 dynamic fractional f strategy (20% as initial active equity) with a daily geometric mean of 1.01933. The time (number of days, since the geometric means are daily) required to double the static fractional f is given by Equation [5.08a] as:

$$\frac{\ln(2)}{\ln(1.005)} = 138.9751$$

To double the dynamic fractional f requires setting the goal to 6. This is because, if you initially have 20% of the equity at work, and you start out with a $100,000 account, then you initially have $20,000 at work. The goal is to make the active equity equal $120,000. Since the inactive equity remains at $80,000, you will have a total of $200,000 on your account that started at $100,000. Thus, to make a $20,000 account grow to $120,000 means you need to achieve a TWR of 6. Therefore, the goal is 6 in order to double a .2 dynamic fractional f:

$$\frac{\ln(6)}{\ln(1.01933)} = 93.58634$$

Notice how it took 93 days for the dynamic fractional f versus 138 days for the static fractional f.

Now let's look at the .1 fraction. The number of days expected in order for the static technique to double is expected as:

$$\frac{\ln(2)}{\ln(1.002577)} = 269.3404$$

If we compare this to doubling a dynamic fractional f which is initially set to .1 active, you need to achieve a TWR of 11. Hence, the number of days required for the comparative dynamic fractional f strategy is:

$$\frac{\ln(11)}{\ln(1.01933)} = 125.2458$$

To double the account equity, at the .1 level of fractional f is, therefore, 269 days for our static example, compared to 125 days for the dynamic. The lower the fraction for f, the faster the dynamic will outperform the static technique.

Let's take a look at tripling the .2 fractional f. The number of days expected by static technique to triple is:

$$\frac{\ln(3)}{\ln(1.005)} = 220.2704$$

This compares to its dynamic counterpart, which requires:

$$\frac{\ln(11)}{\ln(1.01933)} = 125.2458$$

To make 400% profit (i.e., a goal or TWR, of 5) requires of the .2 static technique:

$$\frac{\ln(5)}{\ln(1.005)} = 322.6902$$

Which compares to its dynamic counterpart:

$$\frac{\ln(21)}{\ln(1.01933)} = 159.0201$$

It takes the dynamic almost half the time it takes the static to reach the goal of 400% in this example. However, if you look out in time 322.6902 days to where the static technique doubled, the dynamic technique would be at a TWR of:

$$= .8 + (1.01933 \char`\^ 322.6902) * .2$$

$$= .8 + 482.0659576 * .2$$

$$= 97.21319$$

This represents making over 9,600% in the time it took the static to make 400%.

We can now amend Equation [5.08a] to accommodate both the static and fractional dynamic f strategies to determine the expected length required to achieve a specific goal as a TWR. To begin with, for the static fractional f, we can create Equation [5.08b]:

$$T = \frac{\ln(\text{goal})}{\ln(\text{FGHPR})} \qquad [5.08b]$$

where T = expected number of holding periods to reach a specific goal

goal = goal in terms of a multiple on our starting stake, a TWR

FGHPR = adjusted geometric mean. This is the geometric mean, run through Equation [5.07] to determine the geometric mean for a given static fractional f.

ln( ) = natural logarithm function.

For a dynamic fractional f, we have Equation [5.08c]:

$$T = \frac{\ln\left(\left(\frac{(goal - 1)}{FRAC}\right) + 1\right)}{\ln(\text{geometric mean})} \qquad [5.08c]$$

where T = expected number of holding periods to reach a specific goal.

goal = goal in terms of a multiple on our starting stake, a TWR.

FRAC = initial active equity percentage.

geometric mean = the raw geometric mean HPR at the optimal f; there is no adjustment performed on it as there is in Equation [5.08b].

ln( ) = natural logarithm function.

Thus, to illustrate the use of Equation [5.08c], suppose we want to determine how long it will take an account to double (i.e., TWR = 2) at .1 active equity and a geometric mean of 1.01933:

$$T = \frac{\ln\left(\left(\frac{(goal - 1)}{FRAC}\right) + 1\right)}{\ln(\text{geometric mean})}$$

$$= \frac{\ln\left(\left(\frac{(2 - 1)}{.1}\right) + 1\right)}{\ln(1.01933)}$$

$$= \frac{\ln\left(\frac{(1)}{.1} + 1\right)}{\ln(1.01933)}$$

$$= \frac{\ln(10+1)}{\ln(1.01933)}$$

$$= \frac{\ln(11)}{\ln(1.01933)}$$

$$= \frac{2.397895273}{.01914554872}$$

$$= 125.2455758$$

Thus, if our geometric means are determined off scenarios which have a daily holding period basis, we can expect about 125¼ days to double. If our scenarios used months as holding period lengths, we would have to expect about 125¼ months to double.

As long as you are dealing with a T large enough that Equation [5.08c] is greater than Equation [5.08b], then you are benefiting from dynamic fractional f trading. This can, likewise, be expressed as Equation [5.09]:

$$\text{FGHPR}^T <= \text{geometric mean}^T * \text{FRAC} + 1 - \text{FRAC} \qquad [5.09]$$

Thus, you must iterate to that value of T where the right side of the equation exceeds the left side—that is, the value for T (the number of holding periods) at which you should wait before reallocating, otherwise, you are better off to trade the static fractional f counterpart.

Figure 5.1 illustrates this graphically. The arrow is that value for T at which the left-hand side of Equation [5.09] is equal to the right-hand side.

Thus, if we are using an active equity percentage of 20%, i.e., FRAC = .2, then FGHPR must be figured on the basis of a $.2f$. Thus, for the case where our geometric mean at full optimal f is 1.01933, and the $.2 f$ (FGHPR) is 1.005, we want a value for T which satisfies the following:

$$1.005^T <= 1.01933^T * .2 + 1 - .2$$

We figured our geometric mean for optimal f and, therefore, our geometric mean for the fractional f (FGHPR) on a daily basis, and we want to see if one quarter is enough time. Since there are about sixty-three trading days per quarter, we want to see if a T of sixty-three is enough time to benefit by dynamic fractional f. Therefore, we check Equation [5.09] at a value of sixty-three for T:

$$1.005^{63} <= 1.01933^{63} * .2 + 1 - .2$$

$$1.369184237 <= 3.340663933 * .2 + 1 - .2$$

$$1.369184237 <= .6681327866 + 1 - .2$$

$$1.369184237 <= 1.6681327866 - .2$$

$$1.369184237 <= 1.4681327866$$

The equation is satisfied, since the left side is less than or equal to the right side of the equation. Thus, we can reallocate on a quarterly basis under the given values and benefit from using dynamic fractional f.

Figure 5.1 demonstrates the relationship between trading at a static versus a dynamic fractional f strategy over a period of time.

This chart shows a 20% initial active equity, traded on both a static and a dynamic basis. Since they both start out trading the same number of units, that very same number of units is shown being traded straight through as a constant contract. The geometric mean HPR, at full f used in this chart, was 1.01933; therefore, the geometric mean at the .2 static fractional f was 1.005, and the arithmetic average HPR at full f was 1.0265.

All of this leads to a couple of important points, that the *dynamic fractional* f *will outpace the static fractional f faster, the lower the frac-*

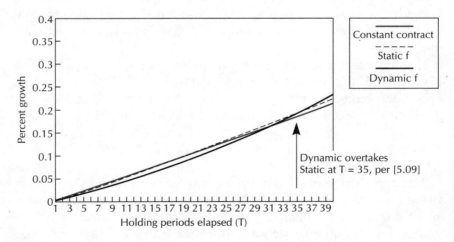

FIGURE 5.1   Percent growth per period for constant contract, static, and dynamic f.

tion and the higher the geometric mean. That is, using an initial active equity percentage of .1 (for both dynamic and static) means that the dynamic will overtake the static faster than if you used a .5 fraction for both. Thus, generally, the dynamic fractional f will overtake its static counterpart faster, the lower the portion of initial active equity. In other words, a portfolio with an initial active equity of .1 will overcome its static counterpart faster than a portfolio with an initial active equity allocation of .2 will overtake its static counterpart. At an initial active equity allocation of 100% (1.0), the dynamic never overtakes the static fractional f (rather, they grow at the same rate). Also affecting the rate at which the dynamic fractional f overtakes its static counterpart is the geometric mean of the portfolio itself. The higher the geometric mean, the sooner the dynamic will overtake its static counterpart. At a geometric mean of 1.0, the dynamic never overtakes its static counterpart.

The more time that elapses, the greater the difference between the static fractional f and the dynamic fractional f strategy. Asymptotically, the dynamic fractional f strategy has infinitely greater wealth than its static counterpart.

One last important point about Figure 5.1. The constant contract line crosses the other two lines before they cross over each other.

In the long run, you are better off to practice asset allocation with a dynamic fractional f technique. That is, you determine an initial level—a percentage—to allocate as active equity. The remainder is inactive equity. The day-to-day equity changes are reflected in the active portion only. The inactive dollar amount remains constant. Therefore, each day you subtract the constant inactive dollar amount from your total account equity. This difference is the active portion, and it is on this active portion that you will figure your quantities to trade in, based on the optimal f levels.

Now, when the margin requirement is calculated for the positions, it will not be exactly the same as your active equity. It can be more or less; it doesn't matter. Thus, unless your margin requirement is for 100% of the equity in the account, you will have some unused cash in the account on any given holding period. Thus, you are almost always inadvertently allocating something to cash (or cash equivalents). So you can see that there isn't any need for a scenario spectrum for cash or cash equivalents—they already get their proper allocation when you do the active and inactive equity split.

REALLOCATION

Notice in Figure 5.1 that, trading at a dynamic fractional f, eventually the active portion of your equity will dwarf the inactive portion, and you will be faced with a portfolio that is far too aggressive for your blood—the same situation you faced in the beginning when you looked at trading the portfolio at the full optimal f amount. Thus, at some point in time in the future, you will want to *reallocate* back to some level of initial active equity.

For instance, you start out at a 10% initial active equity on a $100,000 account. You, therefore, have $10,000 active equity—equity that you are trading full out at the optimal f level. Each day, you will subtract $90,000 from the equity on the account. The difference is the active equity, and it is on the active equity that you trade at the full optimal f levels.

Now, assume that this account got up to $1 million equity. Thus, subtracting the constant dollar inactive amount of $90,000 leaves you at an active equity of $910,000, which means you are now at 91% active equity. Thus, you face those gigantic drawdowns that you sought to avoid initially, when you diluted f and started trading at a 10% initial active equity.

Consider the case of reallocating after every trade or every day. Such is the case with static fractional f trading. Recall again Equation [5.08a], the time required to reach a specific goal.

Let's return to our system that we are trading with a .2 active portion and a geometric mean of 1.01933. We will compare this to trading at the static fractional .2 f, where the resultant geometric mean is 1.005. Now, if we are starting out with a $100,000 account, and we want to reallocate at $110,000 total equity, the number of days (since our geometric means here are on a per-day basis) required by the static fractional .2 f is:

$$\frac{\ln(1.1)}{\ln(1.005)} = 19.10956$$

This compares to using $20,000 of the $100,000 total equity at the full f amount, and trying to get the total account up to $110,000. This would represent a goal of 1.5 times the $20,000:

$$\frac{\ln(1.5)}{\ln(1.01933)} = 21.17807$$

At lower goals, the static fractional f strategy grows faster than its corresponding dynamic fractional f counterpart. As time elapses, the dynamic overtakes the static until, eventually, the dynamic is infinitely further ahead. Figure 5.1 graphically displays this relationship between the static and dynamic fractional fs.

If you reallocate too frequently, you are only shooting yourself in the foot, as the technique would be inferior to its static fractional f counterpart. Therefore, since you are better off, in the long run, to use the dynamic fractional f approach to asset allocation, you are also better off to reallocate funds between the active and inactive subaccounts as infrequently as possible. Ideally, you will only make this division between active and inactive equity once, at the outset of the program.

It is not beneficial to reallocate too frequently. Ideally, you will never reallocate. Ideally, you will let the fraction of optimal f you are using keep approaching 1 as your account equity grows. In reality, however, you most likely will reallocate at some point in time. Hopefully, you will not reallocate so frequently that it becomes a problem.

Reallocation seems to do just the opposite of what we want to do, in that reallocation trims back after a run up in equity, or adds more equity to the active portion after a period in which the equity has been run down.

Reallocation is a compromise. It is a compromise between the theoretical ideal and the real-life implementation. The techniques discussed allow us to make the most of this compromise. Ideally, you would never reallocate. Your humble little $10,000 account, when it grew to $10 million, would never go through reallocation. Ideally, you would sit through the drawdown which took your account down to $50,000 from the $10 million mark before it shot up to $20 million. Ideally, if your active equity were depleted down to one dollar, you would still be able to trade a fractional contract (a *microcontract?*). In an ideal world, all of these things would be possible. In real life, you are going to reallocate at some point on the upside or the downside. Given that you are going to do this, you might as well do it in a systematic, beneficial way.

In reallocating—compromising—you *reset* things back to a state where you would be if you were starting the program all over again, only at a different equity level. Then, you let the outcome of the trading dictate where the fraction of f floats to by using a dynamic fractional f in between reallocations. Things can get levered up awfully fast, even when starting out with an active equity allocation of only 5%. Remember, you are using the full optimal f on this 5%, and if your program does modestly well, you'll be trading in substantial quantities relative to the total equity in the account in short order.

The Mathematics of Money Management detailed four techniques to perform reallocation in ways that may be beneficial to the trader. They will not be reiterated here. Rather, there are a few somewhat important comments which should be stated, and which pertain to reallocation, regardless of the technique.

The first, and perhaps most important, thing to realize about reallocation, at this point in time, can be seen in Figure 5.1. Note the arrow in the figure, which is identified as that T where Equation [5.09] is equal. This amount of time, T, is critical. If you reallocate before T, you are doing yourself harm in trading the dynamic, rather than the static, fractional f.

The next critical thing to realize about reallocation is that you have some control over the maximum drawdown in terms of percentage equity retracements. Notice that you are trading the active portion of an account as though it were an account of exactly that size, full out at the optimal levels. Since you should expect to see nearly 100% equity retracements when trading at the full optimal f levels, you should expect to see 100% of the active equity portion wiped out at any one time.

Further, many traders who have been using the fractional dynamic f approach over the last couple of years relate what appears to be a very good rule of thumb: *Set your initial active equity at one-half of the maximum drawdown you can tolerate.* Thus, if you can take up to a 20% drawdown, set your initial active equity at 10% (however, if the account is profitable and your active equity begins to exceed 20%, you are very susceptible to seeing drawdowns in excess of 20%).

There is a more accurate implementation of this very notion. Notice, that for portfolios, you must use the sum of all f in determining exposure. That is, you must sum the f values up across the components. This is important in that, suppose you have a portfolio comprising of three components, with f values determined, respectively, from the technique detailed in Chapter 4, of .5, .7, and .69. The total of these is 1.89. That is the f you are working with in the portfolio, as a whole. Now, if each of these components saw the worst-case scenario manifest, the account would see a 189% drawdown on active equity! When working with portfolios, you should be very careful to be ever-vigilant for such an event, and to bear this in mind when determining initial active equity allocations.

The third important notion about reallocation pertains to the concept of portfolio insurance and its relationship to optimal f.

PORTFOLIO INSURANCE AND OPTIMAL f

Assume for a moment that you are managing a stock fund. Figure 5.2 depicts a typical portfolio insurance strategy, also known as dynamic hedging. The floor in this example is the current portfolio value of 100 (dollars per share). The typical portfolio will follow the equity market one for one. This is represented by the unbroken line. The insured portfolio is depicted by the dotted line. You will note that the dotted line is below the unbroken line when the portfolio is at its initial value (100) or greater. This difference represents the cost of performing the portfolio insurance. Otherwise, as the portfolio falls in value, portfolio insurance provides a floor on the value of the portfolio at a desired level (in this case, the present value of 100) minus the cost of performing the strategy.

In a nutshell, portfolio insurance is akin to buying a put option on the portfolio. Let's suppose that the fund you are managing consists of only one stock, which is currently priced at $100. Buying a put option on this stock, with a strike price of $100, at a cost of $10, would replicate the dotted line in Figure 5.2. The worst that could happen to your portfolio of one stock and a put option on it is that you could exercise the put, which

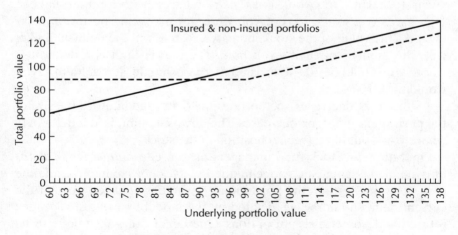

FIGURE 5.2   Portfolio insurance.

sells your stock at $100, and you lose the value of the put, $10. Thus, the worst that this portfolio can be worth is $90, regardless of how far down the underlying stock goes.

On the upside, your insured portfolio suffers somewhat, in that the value of the portfolio is always reduced by the cost of the put.

Now, consider that being long a call option will give you the same profile as being long the underlying and long a put option with the same strike price and expiration date as the call option. When we speak of the same profile, we mean an equivalent position in terms of the risk/reward characteristics at different values for the underlying. Thus, the dotted line in Figure 5.2 can also represent a portfolio composed of simply being long the $100 call option at expiration.

Here is how *dynamic hedging* works to provide portfolio insurance. Suppose you buy 100 shares of this single stock for your fund, at a price of $100 per share. Now, you will replicate the call option by using this underlying stock. The way you will do this is by determining an initial floor for the stock. The floor you choose is, say 100. You also determine an expiration date for this hypothetical option which you are going to create. Let's say that the expiration date you choose is the date on which this quarter ends.

Now, you will figure the delta (the instantaneous rate of change in the price of a call option relative to the change in price of the underlying instrument) for this 100 call option with the chosen expiration date. Suppose the delta is .5. This means that you should be 50% invested in the given stock. Thus, you would only have 50 shares of stock rather than the 100 shares you would have if you were not practicing portfolio insurance. As the value of the stock increases, so, too, will the delta, and likewise the number of shares you hold. The upside limit is a delta at 1, where you would be 100% invested. In our example, at a delta of 1, you would have 100 shares.

As the stock decreases, so, too, does the delta, and likewise the size of the position in the stock decreases. The downside limit is at a delta of 0, where you wouldn't have any position in the stock.

Operationally, stock fund managers have used *noninvasive methods* of dynamic hedging. Such a technique involves not having to trade the cash portfolio. Rather, the portfolio as a whole is adjusted to what the current delta should be, as dictated by the model by using stock index futures, and, sometimes, put options. One benefit of a technique using futures is that futures have low transactions cost.

Selling short futures against the portfolio is equivalent to selling off part of the portfolio and putting it into cash. As the portfolio falls, more futures are sold, and as it rises, these short positions are covered. The loss to the portfolio, as it goes up and the short futures positions are covered, is what accounts for the portfolio insurance cost, the cost of the replicated put options. Dynamic hedging, though, has the benefit of allowing us to closely estimate this cost at the outset. To managers trying to implement such a strategy, it allows the portfolio to remain untouched, while the appropriate asset allocation shifts are performed through futures trades. This noninvasive technique of using futures permits the separation of asset allocation and active portfolio management.

To someone implementing portfolio insurance, you must continuously adjust the portfolio to the appropriate delta. This means that, say, each day, you must input into the option pricing model the current portfolio value, time until expiration, interest rate levels, and portfolio volatility, to determine the delta of the put option you are trying to replicate. Adding this delta (which is a number between 0 and −1) to 1 will give you the corresponding call's delta. This is the hedge ratio, the percentage that you should be investing in the fund.

Suppose your hedge ratio for the present moment is .46. Let's say that the size of the fund you are managing is the equivalent of fifty S&P futures units. Since you only want to be 46% invested, it means you want to be 54% disinvested. Fifty-four percent of fifty units is twenty-seven units. Therefore, at the present price level of the fund at this point in time, for the given interest rate and volatility levels, the fund should be short twenty-seven S&P units along with its long position in cash stocks.

Because the delta needs to be recomputed on an ongoing basis, and portfolio adjustments must be constantly monitored, the strategy is called a dynamic hedging strategy.

One problem with using futures in the strategy is that the futures market does not exactly track the cash market. Further, the portfolio you are selling futures against may not exactly follow the cash index upon which the futures market is traded. These tracking errors can add to the expense of a portfolio insurance program. Furthermore, when the option being replicated gets very near to expiration, and the portfolio value is near the strike price, the gamma of the replicated option goes up astronomically. Gamma is the instantaneous rate of change of the delta or hedge ratio. In other words, gamma is the delta of the delta. If the delta is changing very fast (i.e., if the replicated option has a high gamma), portfolio insurance becomes increasingly more cumbersome to perform. There are numerous ways to work around this problem, some of which are very sophisticated. One of the simplest involves the concept of a perpetual option. For instance, you can always assume that the option you are trying to replicate expires in, say, three months. Each day you will move the replicated option's expiration date ahead by a day. Again, this high gamma usually only becomes a problem when expiration draws near and the portfolio value and the replicated option's strike price are very close.

There is a very interesting relationship between optimal f and portfolio insurance. When you enter a position, you can state that f percent of your funds are invested. For example, consider a gambling game where your optimal f is .5, biggest loss −1, and bankroll is $10,000. In such a case, you would bet one dollar for every two dollars in your stake since −1, the biggest loss, divided by −.5, the negative optimal f, is 2. Dividing $10,000 by 2 yields $5,000. You would, therefore, bet $5,000 on the next bet, which is f percent (50%) of your bankroll. Had we multiplied our bankroll of $10,000 by f (.5), we would have arrived at the same $5,000 result. Hence, we have bet f percent of our bankroll.

Likewise, if our biggest loss were $250 and everything else the same, we would be making one bet for every $500 in our bankroll since −$250/−.5 = $500. Dividing $10,000 by $500 means that we would make twenty bets. Since the most we can lose on any one bet is $250, we have thus risked f percent, 50% of our stake in risking $5,000 ($250 * 20).

Therefore, we can state that f equals the percentage of our funds at risk, or f equals the hedge ratio. Remember, when discussing portfolios, we are discussing the sum of the f values of the components. Since f is only applied on the active portion of our portfolio in a dynamic fractional f strategy, we can state that the hedge ratio of the portfolio, H, equals:

$$H = \left(\sum_{i=1}^{n} f_i \right) * \frac{\text{active\$}}{\text{total equity}} \qquad [5.10a]$$

where H = hedge ratio of the portfolio
             f_i = f value of the ith component in the portfolio
        active\$ = active portion of funds in an account

Equation [5.10a] gives us the hedge ratio for a portfolio being traded on a dynamic fractional f strategy. Portfolio insurance is also at work in a static fractional f strategy, only the quotient active\$/total equity equals 1, and the value for f (the optimal f) is multiplied by whatever value we are using for the fraction of f. Thus, in a static fractional f strategy, the hedge ratio is:

$$H = \left(\sum_{i=1}^{n} f_i \right) * \text{FRAC} \qquad [5.10\text{b}]$$

We can state that in trading an account on a dynamic fractional f basis, we are performing portfolio insurance. Here, the floor is known in advance and is equal to the initial inactive equity plus the cost of performing the insurance. However, it is often simpler to refer to the floor of a dynamic fractional f strategy as the initial inactive equity of an account.

We can state that Equation [5.10a or b] equals the delta of the call option of the terms used in portfolio insurance. Further, we find that this delta changes much the way a call option, which is deep out of the money and very far from expiration, changes. Thus, by using a constant inactive dollar amount, trading an account on a dynamic fractional f strategy is equivalent to owning a put option on the portfolio which is deep in the money and very far out in time. Equivalently, we can state that trading a dynamic fractional f strategy is the same as owning a call option on the portfolio which doesn't expire for a very long time and is very far out of the money.

However, it is also possible to use portfolio insurance as a reallocation technique to steer performance somewhat. This steering may be analogous to trying to steer a tanker with a rowboat oar, but this is a valid reallocation technique. The method initially involves setting parameters for the program. First, you must determine a floor value. Once chosen, you must decide upon an expiration date, volatility level, and other input parameters to the particular option model you intend to use. These inputs will give you the option's delta at any given point in time. Once the delta is known, you can determine what your active equity should be. Since the delta for the account, the variable H in Equation [5.10a], must equal the delta for the call option being replicated:

$$H = \left(\sum_{i=1}^{n} f_i \right) * \frac{\text{active\$}}{\text{total equity}}$$

Therefore:

$$\frac{H}{\displaystyle\sum_{i=1}^{n} f_i} = \frac{\text{active\$}}{\text{total equity}} \quad \text{if } H < \sum_{i=1}^{n} f_i \qquad [5.11]$$

otherwise
$$H = \frac{\text{active\$}}{\text{total equity}} = 1$$

Since active\$/total equity is equal to the percentage of active equity, we can state that the percentage of funds we should have in active equity, of the total account equity, is equal to the delta on the call option divided by the sum of the f values of the components. However, you will note that if H is greater than the sum of these f values, then it is suggesting that you allocate greater than 100% of an account's equity as active. Since this is not possible, there is an upper limit of 100% of the account's equity that can be used as active equity.

Portfolio insurance is great in theory, but poor in practice. As witnessed in the 1987 stock market crash, the problem with portfolio insurance is that, when prices plunge, there isn't any liquidity at any price. This does not concern us here, however, since we are looking at the relationship between active and inactive equity, and how this is mathematically similar to portfolio insurance.

The problem with implementing portfolio insurance as a reallocation technique, as detailed here, is that reallocation is taking place constantly. This detracts from the fact that a dynamic fractional f strategy will asymptotically dominate a static fractional f strategy. As a result, trying to steer performance by way of portfolio insurance as a dynamic fractional f reallocation strategy probably isn't such a good idea. However, anytime you use fractional f, static or dynamic, you are employing a form of portfolio insurance.

UPSIDE LIMIT ON ACTIVE EQUITY AND THE MARGIN CONSTRAINT

Here is a problem which continuously crops up when we take any of the fixed fractional trading techniques out of their theoretical context and apply them in a real-world sense. *The Mathematics of Money Manage-*

ment showed that anytime an additional market system is added to a portfolio, as long as that market system's linear correlation coefficient of daily equity changes to another market system's in the portfolio is less than +1, the portfolio is improved. That is to say, the geometric mean of daily HPRs is increased. Thus, it stands to reason that you would want to have as many market systems as possible in a portfolio. Naturally, at some point, margin considerations become a problem.

Even if you are trading only one market system, margin considerations can often be a problem. Consider that the optimal f in dollars is very often less than the initial margin requirement for a given market. Now, depending on what fraction of f you are using at the moment, whether you are using a static or dynamic fractional f strategy, you will encounter a margin call if the fraction is too high.

When you trade a portfolio of market systems, the problem of a margin call becomes even more likely.

What is needed is a way to reconcile how to create an optimal portfolio within the bounds of the margin requirements on the components in the portfolio. This can very easily be found. The way to accomplish this is to find what fraction of f you can use as an upper limit. This upper limit, L, is given by Equation [5.12]:

$$L = \frac{\overset{n}{\underset{i=1}{MAX}}(f_i\$)}{\sum_{k=1}^{n}\left(\left(\overset{n}{\underset{i=1}{MAX}}(f_i\$)\middle/f_k\$\right) * \text{margin}_k\right)} \qquad [5.12]$$

where
L = upside fraction of f. At this particular fraction of f, you are trading the optimal portfolio as aggressively as possible without incurring an initial margin call.

$f_k\$$ = optimal f in dollars for the kth market system.

$\text{margin}_k\$$ = initial margin requirement of the kth market system.

n = total number of market systems in the portfolio.

Equation [5.12] is really much simpler than it appears. For starters, in both the numerator and the denominator, we find the expression $\overset{n}{\underset{i=1}{MAX}}$, which simply means to take the greatest $f\$$ of all of the components in the portfolio.

Let's assume a two-component portfolio, which we'll call spectrum A and B. We can arrange the necessary information for determining the upside limit on active equity in a table as follows:

Component	$f\$$	Margin	Greatest $f\$/f\$$
Spectrum A	$2,500	$11,000	2500/2500 = 1
Spectrum B	$1,500	$2,000	2500/1500 = 1.67

Now we can plug these values into Equation [5.12]. Notice that $\overset{n}{\underset{i=1}{MAX}}$ is $2,500, since the only other $f\$$ is $1,500, which is less. Thus:

$$L = \frac{2500}{1 * 11000 + 1.67 * 2000} = \frac{2500}{11000 + 3340} = \frac{2500}{14,340} = 17.43375174\%$$

This tells us that 17.434% should be our maximum upside percentage.

Now, suppose we had a $100,000 account. If we were at 17.434% active equity, we would have $17,434 in active equity. Thus, assuming we can trade in fractional units for the moment, we would buy 6.9736 (17,434/2,500) of Spectrum A and 11.623 (17,434/1,500) of Spectrum B. The margin requirements on this would then be:

$$6.9726 * 11,000 = \quad 76,698.60$$

$$11.623 * 2,000 = \quad 23,245.33$$

Total Margin Requirement = $99,943.93

If, however, we are still employing a static fractional f strategy (despite this author's protestations), then the highest you should set that fraction is 17.434%. This will result in the same margin call as above.

Notice that using Equation [5.12] yields the highest fraction for f without incurring an initial margin call that gives you the same ratios of the different market systems to one another.

Chapter 2 of *The Mathematics of Money Management* explained the fact that adding more and more market systems (scenario spectrums) results in higher and higher geometric means for the portfolio as a whole. However, there is a tradeoff in that each market system adds marginally less benefit to the geometric mean, but marginally more detriment in the way of efficiency loss due to simultaneous rather than sequential outcomes. Therefore, we have seen that you do not want to trade an infinitely high number of scenario spectrums. What's more, theoretically optimal portfolios run into the real-life application problem of margin constraints. In other words, you are usually better off to trade three scenario spectrums at the full optimal f levels than to trade 10 at dramatically reduced levels as a result of Equation [5.12]. Usually, you will find that the optimal number of scenario spectrums to trade in, particularly when you have many orders to place and the potential for mistakes, is but a handful.

STOCK TRADING

The techniques which have been described in this book not only apply to futures traders, but to traders in any market. Even to someone trading a portfolio of only blue chip stocks is not immune from the principles and the consequences discussed in this book. You have seen that such a portfolio of blue chip stocks has an optimal level of leverage (with *both* of its meanings) where the ratio of potential gains to potential losses in equity are maximized. At such a level, the drawdowns to be expected are also quite severe, and, therefore, the portfolio ought to be diluted, preferably by way of a dynamic fractional f strategy.

In dealing with stocks, the margin requirement can be either the margin requirement (if done in a margin account), or the actual price of the stocks if performed in a cash account. That is, if a stock is $40 per share, then the cost of *margining* 100 shares in a cash account is $4,000.

f SHIFT AND CONSTRUCTING A ROBUST PORTFOLIO

Earlier in this text, mention was made of the polymorphic nature of the $n + 1$ dimensional landscape; that is, the landscape is undulating—the peak in the landscape tends to move around as the markets and techniques we use to trade them change in character. This f shift is doubtless a problem to all traders. Oftentimes, if the f shift is towards zero for many axes—that is, as the scenario spectrums weaken—it can cause what would otherwise be a winning method on a constant unit basis to be a losing program because the trader is beyond the peak of the f curve (to the right of the peak) to an extent that he is in a losing position.

f shift exists in all markets and approaches. It frequently occurs to the point at which many scenario spectrums get allocations in one period in an optimal portfolio construction, then no allocations in the period immediately following. This tells us that the performance, out of sample, tends to greatly diminish. The reverse is also true. Markets that appear as poor candidates in one period where an optimal portfolio is determined, then come on strong in the period immediately following, since the scenarios do not measure up.

When constructing scenarios and scenario sets, you should pay particular attention to this characteristic: Markets that have been performing well will tend to underperform in the next period and vice versa. Bearing this in mind when constructing your scenarios and scenario spectrums will help you to develop more robust portfolios, and help alleviate f shift.

TAILORING A TRADING PROGRAM THROUGH REALLOCATION

Often, money managers may opt for the dynamic f, as opposed to the static, even when the number of holding periods is less than that specified by Equation [5.09], simply because the dynamic provides a better implementation of portfolio insurance.

In such cases, it is important that the money manager not reallocate until Equation [5.09] is satisfied—that is, until enough holding periods elapse that the dynamic can begin to outperform the static counterpart.

A real key to tailoring trading programs to fit the money manager's goals in these instances is by reallocating on the upside. That is, at some upside point in active equity, you should reallocate to achieve a certain goal, yet that point is beyond some minimum point in time (i.e., number of elapsed holding periods).

Returning to Figure 5.1, Equation [5.09] gives us T, or where the crossing of the static f line by the dynamic f line occurs with respect to the horizontal coordinate. That is the point, in terms of number of elapsed holding periods, at which we obtain more benefit from trading the dynamic f rather than the static f. However, once we know T from Equation [5.09], we can figure the Y, or vertical, axis where the points cross as:

$$Y = \text{FRAC} * \text{geometric mean}^T - \text{FRAC} \qquad [5.13]$$

where
T = variable T derived from Equation [5.09]
FRAC = initial active portion of funds in an account
geometric mean = raw geometric mean HPR; there is no adjustment performed on it as there is in Equation [5.08b]

Example:

Initial Active Equity Percentage = 5% (i.e., .05)
Geomean HPR per period = 1.004171
$T = 316$

We know at 316 periods, on average, the dynamic will begin to out-perform the corresponding static *f* for the same value of *f*, per Equation [5.09]. This is the same as saying that, starting at an initial active equity of 5%, when the account is up by 13.63% (.05 * 1.004171^{316} − .05), the dynamic will begin to outperform the corresponding static *f* for the same value of *f*.

So, we can see that there is a minimum number of holding periods which must elapse in order for the dynamic fractional *f* to overtake its static counterpart (*prior to which, reallocation is harmful if implementing the dynamic fractional f, and, after which, it is harmful to trade the static fractional f*), which can also be converted from a horizontal point to a vertical one. That is, rather than a minimum number of holding periods, a minimum profit objective can be used.

Reallocating when the equity equals or exceeds this target of active equity will generally result in a much smoother equity curve than reallocating based on *T,* the horizontal axis. That is, most money managers will find it advantageous to reallocate based on upside progress rather than elapsed holding periods.

What is most interesting here is that for a given level of initial active equity, the upside target will always be the same, regardless of what values you are using for the geometric mean HPR or T! Thus, a 5% initial active equity level will always see the dynamic overtake the static at a 13.63% profit on the account!

Since we have an optimal upside target, we can state that there is, as well, an optimal delta on the portfolio on the upside. So, what is the formula for the optimal upside delta? This can be discerned by Equations [5.10a and b], where FRAC equals that fraction of active equity which would be seen by satisfying Equation [5.13]. This is given as:

$$FRAC = \frac{(\text{Initial Active Equity} + \text{Upside Target})}{(1 + \text{Upside Target})} \quad [5.14]$$

Thus, if we start out with an initial active equity of 5%, then 13.63% is the upside point where the dynamic would be expected to overtake the static, and we would use the following for FRAC in Equations [5.10a and b] in determining the hedge ratio at the upside point, Y, dictated by Equation [5.13]:

$$\text{FRAC} = \frac{(.05 + .1363)}{(1 + .1363)}$$

$$= \frac{.1863}{1.1363}$$

$$= .1639531814$$

Thus, when we have an account which is up 13.63%, and we start with a 5% initial active equity, we know that the active equity is then 16.39531814%.

GRADIENT TRADING AND CONTINUOUS DOMINANCE

We have seen throughout this text, as well as in the two earlier texts, that trading at the optimal f for a given market system or scenario spectrum (or the set of optimal fs for multiple simultaneous scenario spectrums or market systems) will yield the greatest growth asymptotically, that is, in the long run, as the number of holding periods we trade for gets greater and greater. However, we have seen in Chapter 2 that if we have a finite number of holding periods and we know how many holding periods we are going to trade for, what is truly optimal is somewhat more aggressive even than the optimal f values; that is, it is those values for f which maximize expected average compound growth (EACG).

Ultimately, each of us can only trade a finite number of holding periods—none of us will live forever. Yet, in all but the rarest cases, we do not know the exact length of that finite number of holding periods, so we use the asymptotic limit as the next best approximation.

Now you will see, however, a technique that can be used in this case of an unknown, but finite, number of holding periods over which you are going to trade at the asymptotic limit (i.e., the optimal f values), which, if you are trading any kind of a diluted f (static or dynamic), allows for dominance not only asymptotically, but for *any given holding period in the future*.

That is, we will now introduce a technique for a diluted f (which nearly all money managers must use in order to satisfy the real-world demands of clients pertaining to drawdowns) that not only ensures that an account will be at the highest equity in the very long run sense, but ensures that it

will be at the highest equity at any point in time, however near or far into the future that is! No longer must someone adhering to optimal f (or, in a broader sense, this new framework) reconcile themselves with the notion that it will be dominant in the long run. Rather, the techniques about to be illustrated seek dominance at all points in time!

This is a gigantic leap. Since nearly everyone will be diluting what their optimal f values are—either intentionally, or unintentionally through ignorance—these techniques always maximize the profitability of an account in cases of diluted f values, not just, as has always been the case with geometric mean maximization, in the very long run.

Again, we must turn our attention to growth functions and rates. Look at Figure 5.3, where growth (the growth functions) is represented as a percentage of our starting stake. Now consider Figure 5.4, which shows the growth rate as a percentage of our stake.

Again, these charts show a 20% initial active equity, traded on both a static and a dynamic basis. Since they both start out trading the same number of units, that very same number of units is shown being traded straight through as a constant contract. The geometric mean HPR (at full f) used in this chart was 1.01933; therefore, the geometric mean at the .2 static fractional f was 1.005, and the arithmetic average HPR at full f was 1.0265.

Notice that by always trading that technique which has the highest gradient at the moment, we ensure the probability of the account being at its greatest equity at any point in time. Thus, we start out trading on a con-

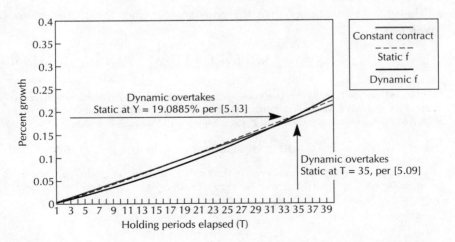

FIGURE 5.3 Points where one method overtakes another can be viewed with respect to time or return.

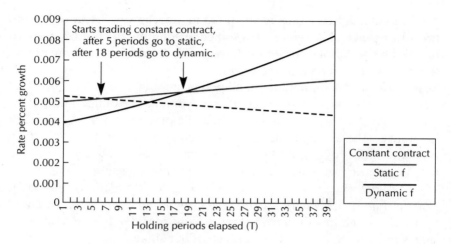

FIGURE 5.4 Growth rate as a percentage of stake.

stant contract basis, with the number of units being determined as that number which would be traded initially if we were trading a fractional *f*.

Next, the static *f* gradient dominates, at which point in time (or on the upside in equity) we switch to trading the static *f*. Finally, the dynamic gradient dominates, at which point we switch to trading on a dynamic *f* basis. Notice that by always trading that technique which has the highest gradient at that moment means you will be on the highest of the three lines in Figure 5.3.

The growth function, *Y*, for the constant contract technique is now given as:*

$$Y = 1 + (AHPR - 1) * FRAC * T \qquad [5.15]$$

---

* Just as Equation [5.09] gave us that point where the dynamic overtakes the static with respect to the horizontal axis *T*, we can determine from Equations [5.15] and [5.16] where the static overtakes a constant contract as that value of *T* where Equation [5.16] equals Equation [5.15]:

$$1 + (AHPR - 1) * FRAC * T => FGHPR^T$$

Likewise, this can be expressed in terms of the *Y* coordinate, to tell us at what percentage of profit, on the total equity in the account, we should switch from a constant contract to static *f* trading:

$$Y = FGHPR^T - 1$$

The value for *T* used in the preceding equation is derived from the one above it.

The growth functions are taken from Equation [5.09]. Thus, the static f growth function is the left side of [5.09], and the dynamic f is the right side. Thus, the growth function for static f is:

$$Y = FGHPR^T \qquad [5.16]$$

And for dynamic f, it is:

$$Y = \text{geometric mean}^T * FRAC + 1 - FRAC \qquad [5.17]$$

Equations [5.15–17] give us the growth function as a multiple of our starting stake, at a given number of elapsed holding periods, T. Thus, by subtracting 1 from Equations [5.15–17], we obtain the percent growth as depicted in Figure 5.3.

The gradients, depicted in Figure 5.4, are simply the first derivatives of Y with respect to T, for Equations [5.15–17]. Thus, the gradients are given by the following.

For constant contract trading:

$$\frac{dY}{dT} = \frac{((AHPR - 1) * FRAC)}{(1 + AHPR - 1) * FRAC * T} \qquad [5.18]$$

For static fractional f:

$$\frac{dY}{dT} = FGHPR^T * \ln(FGHPR) \qquad [5.19]$$

And finally for dynamic fractional f:

$$\frac{dY}{dT} = \text{geometric mean}^T * \ln(\text{geometric mean}) * FRAC \qquad [5.20]$$

where T = number of holding periods
FRAC = initial active equity percentage
geometric mean = raw geometric mean HPR at the optimal f
AHPR = arithmetic average HPR at full optimal f
FGHPR = fractional f geometric mean HPR given by Equation [5.07]
$\ln(\ )$ = natural logarithm function

The way to implement these equations, especially as your scenarios (scenario spectrums) and joint probabilities change from holding period to holding period, is as follows. Recall that just before each holding period we must determine the optimal allocations. In the exercise of doing that, we derive all of the necessary information to get the values for the variables listed above (for FRAC, geometric mean, AHPR, and the inputs to Equation [5.07] to determine the FGHPR). Next, we plug these values into Equations [5.18], [5.19], and [5.20]. Whichever of these three equations results in the greatest value is the technique we go with.

To illustrate by way of an example, we now return to our familiar two-to-one coin toss. Let's assume that this is our only scenario set, comprising the two scenarios heads and tails. Further, suppose we are going to trade it at a .2 fraction (i.e., one-fifth optimal f). Thus FRAC is .2, the geometric mean is 1.06066, and the AHPR is 1.125. To figure the FGHPR, from Equation [5.07], we already have FRAC and AHPR; we only need SD, the standard deviation in HPRs, which is .375. Thus, the FGHPR is

$$1.022252415 = \left(\sqrt{((1.125 - 1)*.2 + 1)^2 - (.375*.2)^2}\right)$$

Plugging these values into the three gradient functions, Equations [5.18–20], gives us the following table:

	Eq. [5.18]	Eq. [5.19]	Eq. [5.20]
T	Constant Contract	Static f	Dynamic f
1	0.024390244	0.022498184	0.012492741
2	0.023809524	0.022998823	0.013250551
3	0.023255814	0.023510602	0.014054329
4	0.022727273	0.02403377	0.014906865
5	0.022222222	0.024568579	0.015811115
6	0.02173913	0.025115289	0.016770217
7	0.021276596	0.025674165	0.017787499
8	0.020833333	0.026245477	0.018866489
9	0.020408163	0.026829503	0.02001093
10	0.02	0.027426524	0.021224793
11	0.019607843	0.02803683	0.022512289
12	0.019230769	0.028660717	0.023877884
13	0.018867925	0.029298488	0.025326317

14	0.018518519	0.02995045	0.026862611
15	0.018181818	0.030616919	0.028492097
16	0.017857143	0.03129822	0.030220427
17	0.01754386	0.031994681	0.032053599
18	0.017241379	0.03270664	0.03399797
19	0.016949153	0.033434441	0.036060287
20	0.016666667	0.034178439	0.038247704

We find that we are at the greatest gradient for the first two holding periods by trading on a constant contract basis, and that on the third period, we should switch to static f. On the seventeenth period, we should switch to dynamic f. If we were to do this, Figure 5.5 shows how much better we would have fared, on average, over the first twenty plays or holding periods, than by simply trading a dynamic fractional f strategy:

Notice that, at every period, an account traded this way has a higher expected value than even the dynamic fractional f. Further, from period 17 on, where we switched from static to dynamic, both lines are forevermore on the same gradient. That is, the dynamic line will never be able to catch up to the continuous dominance line. Thus, the principle of always trading the highest gradient to achieve continuous dominance helps a money manager maximize where an account will be at any point in the future, not just in an asymptotic sense.

To clarify by carrying the example further, suppose we play this two-to-one coin toss game, and we start out with an account of $200. Our

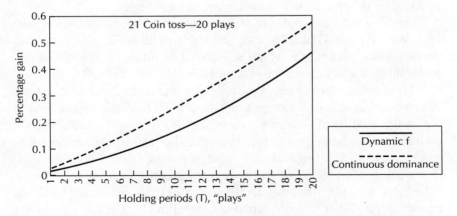

FIGURE 5.5 Continuous dominance vs. dynamic f.

optimal f is .25, and a .2 f, one-fifth of this, means we are trading an f value of .05, or we bet one dollar for every twenty dollars in our stake. Therefore, on the first play we bet ten dollars. Since we are trading constant contract, regardless of where the account equity is thereafter, we bet ten dollars on each subsequent play until we switch over to static f. This occurs on the third play. So, on the third bet, we take where our stake is, and bet one dollar for every twenty dollars we have in equity. We proceed as such through play 16, where, going into the seventeenth play, we will switch over to dynamic. Thus, as we go into every play, from play 3 through play 16, we divide our total equity by twenty dollars and bet that many dollars, thus performing a static fractional f.

So, assume that after the second play we have $210 in our stake. We would now bet ten dollars on the next play (since 210/20 = 10.5, and we must round down to the integer). We keep doing this going into each play through the sixteenth play.

On the seventeenth play, we can see that the dynamic f gradient overtakes the others, so we must now switch over to trading on a dynamic f basis. Here is how. When we started, we decided that we were going to trade a 20% active equity, in effect (because we decided to trade at one-fifth the full optimal f). Since our starting stake was $200, then it means we would have started out, going into play 1, with $40 active equity. We would therefore have $160 inactive equity.

So, going into play 17, where we want to switch over to dynamic, we subtract $160 from whatever is our equity. The difference we then divide by $4, the optimal f $, and that is how many bets we make on play 17. We proceed by doing this before each play, ad infinitum.

Therefore, let's assume our stake stood at $292 after the sixteenth play. We subtract $160 from this, leaving us with $132, which we then divide by the optimal f $, which is $4, for a result of 33. We would thus make thirty-three bets on the seventeenth play (i.e., bet $33).

If you prefer, you can also figure these continuous dominance breakpoints as an upside percentage gain which must be made before switching to the next level. Just as Equation [5.13] gives us the vertical, or Y, coordinate corresponding to Equation [5.09]'s horizontal coordinate, we can determine the vertical coordinates corresponding to Equations [5.18–20]. Since you move from a constant contract to static f at that value of T whereby Equation [5.19] is greater than Equation [5.18], you can then plug that T into Equation [5.16], and subtract 1 from the answer. This is the percentage gain on your starting equity required to switch from a constant contract to static f.

Since you move to dynamic *f* from static *f* at that value of *T* whereby Equation [5.20] is greater than Equation [5.19], you can then plug that value for *T* into Equation [5.17], subtract 1 from the answer, and that is the percentage profit from your starting equity to move to trading on a dynamic *f* basis.

IMPORTANT POINTS TO THE LEFT OF THE PEAK IN THE *n* + 1 DIMENSIONAL LANDSCAPE

We continue this discussion that is directed towards most money managers, who will trade a diluted *f* set; that is, they will trade at less aggressive levels than optimal for the different scenario spectrums or market systems they are employing. We refer to this as being to the *left,* a term which comes from the idea that, if we were looking at trading one scenario spectrum, we would have one curve drawn out in two-dimensional space, where being to the left of the peak corresponds to having less units on a trade than is optimal. If we are trading two scenario spectrums, we have a topographical map in three-dimensional space, where such money managers would restrict themselves to that real estate which is to the left of the peak when looking from south to north at the landscape, and left of the peak when looking from east to west at the landscape. We could carry the thought into more dimensions, but the term *to the left,* is irrespective of the number of dimensions; it simply means at less than full optimal with respect to each axis (scenario spectrum).

Money managers are *not* wealth maximizers. That is, their utility function or, rather, the utility functions imposed on them by their clients and their industry, their $U''(x)$, is less than 0. They are, therefore, to the left of the peaks of their optimal *f*s.

Thus, given the real-world constraints of smoother equity curves than full optimal calls for, as well as the realization that a not-so-typical drawdown at the optimal level will surely cause a money manager's clients to flee, we are faced with the prospect of where, to the left, is an opportune point (to satisfy their $U''(x)$)? Once this opportune point is found, we can then exercise continuous dominance. In so doing, we will be ensuring that by trading at this opportune point to the left, we will have the highest expected value for the account at any point thereafter. It does not mean, however, that it will outpace an account traded at the full optimal *f* set. It will not.

Now we actually begin to work with this new framework. Hence, the point of this section is twofold: first, to point out that there are possible advantageous points to the left, and, second, but more importantly, to show you, by way of examples, how the new framework can be used.

There are a number of advantageous points to the left of the peak, and what follows is not exhaustive. Rather, it is a starting place for you.

The first point of interest to the left pertains to constant contract trading, that is, always trading in the same unit size regardless of where equity runs up or shrinks. This should not be dismissed as overly simplistic by candidate money managers for the following reason: *Always trading the same constant quantity, regardless of account equity, maximizes the probability that a profitable system will be profitable in the future. Varying the trading quantity relative to account equity attempts to maximize the profitability (yet it does not maximize the probability of being profitable).*

The problem with trading the same constant quantity is that it not only puts you to the left of the peak, but, as the account equity grows, you are actually migrating towards zero on the various f axes.

For instance, let's assume we are playing the two-to-one coin toss game. The peak is at $f = .25$, or making one bet for every four dollars in account equity. Let's say we have a twenty dollar account, and we plan to always make two bets, i.e., to always bet two dollars regardless of where the equity goes. Thus, we start out (fortunately, this is a two-dimensional case since we are only discussing one scenario spectrum) trading at an $f\$$ of ten dollars, which is an f of .1, since $f\$ = -BL/f$, it follows that $f = -BL/f\$$. Now, let us assume that we continue to always bet two dollars; that if the account were to get to thirty dollars total equity, our f, given that we are still only betting two dollars, corresponding to an $f\$$ of fifteen dollars, has migrated to .067. As the account continues to make money, the f we are employing would continue to migrate left. However, it also works in reverse—that, if we are losing money, the f we are employing migrates right, and at some point may actually round over the peak of the landscape. Thus, the peak represents where a constant contract trader should stop constant contract trading on the downside. Thus, the f is migrating around, passing through other points in the landscape, some of which are still to be discussed.

Another approach is to begin by defining the worst case drawdown the money manager can afford, in terms of percentage equity retracements, and use that in lieu of the optimal f in determining $f\$$.

$$f\$ = \frac{\text{abs(biggest loss scenario)}}{\text{maximum drawdown percent}} \qquad [5.21a]$$

Thus, if the maximum tolerable drawdown to a money manager is 20%, and the worst-case scenario calls for a loss of –$1,000:

$$f\$ = \frac{\$1,000}{.2} = \$5,000$$

He should thus use $5,000 for his $f\$$. In doing so, he still does not restrict his worst-case drawdown to 20% retracement on equity. Rather, what he has accomplished is that the drawdown to be experienced with the manifestation of the single catastrophic event is defined in advance.

Note that in using this technique, the money manager must make certain that the maximum drawdown percent is not greater than the optimal f, or this technique will put him to the right of the peak. For instance, if the optimal f is actually .1, but the money manager uses this technique with a .2 value for maximum drawdown percentage, he will then be trading an $f\$$ of $5,000 when he should be trading an $f\$$ of $10,000 at the optimal level! Trouble is certain to befall him.

Further, the example given only shows for trading one scenario spectrum. If you are trading more than one scenario spectrum, you must change your denominator to reflect this, dividing the maximum drawdown percent by n, the number of scenario spectrums:

$$f\$ = \frac{\text{abs(biggest loss scenario)}}{\left(\dfrac{\text{maximum drawdown percent}}{n} \right)} \qquad [5.21b]$$

where n = number of components (scenario spectrums or market systems) in the portfolio

Notice that by doing this, if each scenario spectrum realizes its worst-case scenario simultaneously, you will still have defined the maximum drawdown percent for the entire portfolio.

Next, we move on to another important point to the left, which may be of importance to certain money managers: the *growth risk ratio*, or GRR (Figure 5.6). If we take the TWR as the growth, the numerator, and the f used (or the sum of the f values used for portfolios) as representing risk, since it represents the percentage of your stake you would lose if the worst case scenarios(s) manifest, then we can write the growth risk ratio as:

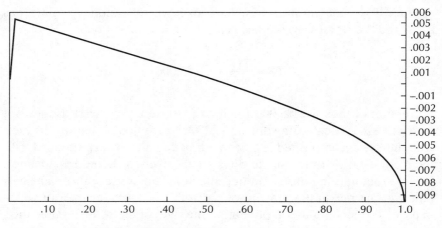

FIGURE 5.6   Two-to-one coin toss, GRR at $T = 1$.

$$\mathrm{GRR}_T = \frac{\mathrm{TWR}_T}{\displaystyle\sum_{i=1}^{n} f_i} \qquad\qquad [5.22]$$

This ratio is exactly what its name implies, the ratio of growth (TWR_T, the expected multiple on our stake after T plays) to risk (sum of the f values, which represent the total percentage of our stake risked). If TWR is a function of T, then too is the GRR. That is, as T increases, the GRR moves from that point where it is an infinitesimally small value for f, towards the optimal f (see Figure 5.7). At infinite T, the GRR equals the optimal f. Much like the EACG, you can trade at the f value to maximize the GRR if you know, a priori, what value for T you are trying to maximize for.

The migration from an infinitesimally small value for f at $T = 1$ to the optimal f at T = infinity happens with respect to all axes, although in Figures 5.6 and 5.7 it is shown for trading one scenario spectrum. If you were trading two scenario spectrums simultaneously, the peak of the GRR would migrate through the three-dimensional landscape as T increased, from nearly 0,0 for both values of f, to the optimal values for f (at .23,.23 in the two-to-one coin toss).

Discerning the GRR for more than one scenario spectrum traded simultaneously is simple, using Equation [5.22], regardless of how many multiple simultaneous scenario spectrums we are looking at.

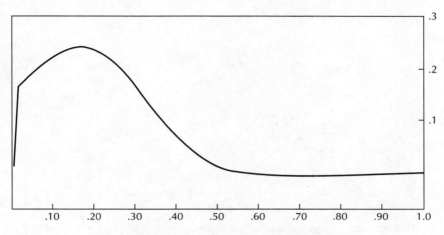

FIGURE 5.7   Two-to-one coin toss, GRR at $T = 30$.

The next and final point to be covered to the left, which may be quite advantageous for many money managers, is the point of inflection in the TWR with respect to f.

Refer again to Figure 1.2 on page 16. Notice that as we approach the peak in the optimal f from the left, starting at 0, we gain TWR (vertical) at an ever-increasing rate, up to a point. We are thus getting greater and greater benefit for a linear increase in risk. However, at a certain point, the TWR curve gains, but at a slower and slower rate for every increase in f. This point of changeover, called *inflection,* because it represents where the function goes from concave up to concave down, is another important point to the left for the money manager. The point of inflection represents the point where the marginal increase in gain stops increasing and actually starts to diminish for every marginal increase in risk. Thus, it may be an extremely important point for a money manager, and may even, in some cases, be optimal in the eyes of the money manager in the sense of what it does, in fact, maximize.

However, recall that Figure 1.2 represents the TWR after forty plays. Let's look at the TWR after one play for the two-to-one coin toss, also simply called the geometric mean HPR, as shown in Figure 5.8.

Interestingly, there isn't any point here where the function goes from concave up to concave down, or vice versa. There aren't any points of inflection. The whole thing is concave down.

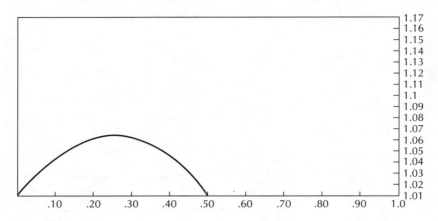

FIGURE 5.8   Geometric mean HPR two-to-one coin toss (= TWR at $T = 1$).

For a positive arithmetic expectation, the geometric mean does not have any points of inflection. However, the TWR, if $T > 1$, has two points of inflection, one to the left of the peak and one to the right. The one which concerns us is, of course, the one to the left of the peak.

The left point of inflection is nonexistent at $T = 1$ and, as T increases, it approaches the optimal f from the left (Figures 5.9 and 5.10). When T is infinite, the point of inflection converges upon optimal f.

Unfortunately, the left point of inflection migrates towards optimal f as T approaches infinity, just like with the GRR. Again, just like EACG,

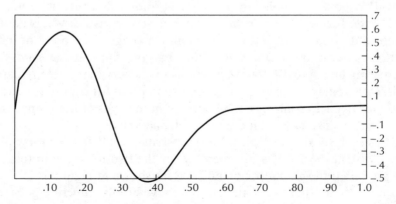

FIGURE 5.9 dTWR/df for 40 plays ($T = 40$) of the two-to-one coin toss. The peak to the left, and the trough to the right, are the points of inflection.

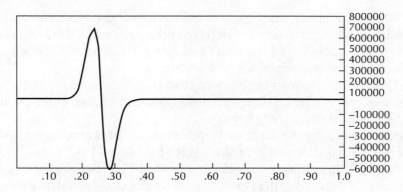

FIGURE 5.10 dTWR/df for 800 plays (T = 800) of the two-to-one coin toss. The peak to the left, and the trough to the right, are the points of inflection. The left peak is at f = .23.

if you knew how many finite T you were to trade before you started trading, you could maximize the left point of inflection.*

To recap how the left point of inflection migrates towards optimal f, the following table depicts the numbers for the two-to-one coin toss game:

2:1 Coin Toss

# plays (T)	f inflection left
1	0
30	.12
40	.13
80	.17
800	.23

Thus, we again see that, as more time elapses, as T increases, missing the optimal f carries with it a steep penalty. Asymptotically, nearly everything is maximized, whether it is EACG, GRR, or the left point of inflection. As T increases, they all converge on optimal f. Thus, as T increases, the distance between these advantageous points and optimal f diminishes.

---

* Interestingly though, if you were trying to maximize the EACG for a given T, you would be seeking a point to the *right* of the peak of the f curve, as the f value which maximizes EACG migrates towards the optimal f as T approaches infinity from the *right*.

Suppose a money manager uses daily HPRs and wants to be optimal (with respect to inflection or GRR) over the course of the current quarter (63 days). He would use a value of 63 for T and set himself at those coordinates to be optimal for each quarter.

When we begin working in more than two dimensions, i.e., when we are dealing with more than one scenario spectrum, we enter an altogether more complicated problem.

The solution can be expressed mathematically as that point where the second partial derivatives of the TWR (Equation [4.04], raised to the power of T, the number of holding periods at which we are seeking the points of inflection) with respect to a each particular f equals 0, and each point is to the left (on its axis) of the peak. This becomes ever more complicated in that such a point, where the second partials of the TWR with respect to each f equaling zero may not, depending upon the parameters of the scenario spectrums themselves and how high or low T is, exist. If T equals 1, the TWR equals the geometric mean HPR, which is upside down parabolic—it doesn't have any points of inflection! Yet as T approaches infinity, the point(s) of inflection approach the optimal $f(s)$! Shy of infinite T, there may not be in most cases, such a conveniently common point of inflection with respect to all axes.*

All of this brings us right back to the beginning of the book. The entire notion of the $n + 1$ dimensional terrain in leverage space, if you will, the axes of which correspond to the f values of the different scenario sets, is to act as a *framework* for analyzing portfolio construction and quantity determination through time. There is so much more to be done in working with this new framework. This book is not the end-all on the subject. Rather, it is a mere introduction to an altogether new and, I believe, better way of determining asset allocation. Almost certainly, portfolio strategists, applied mathematicians, asset allocators, and programmers have much new fertile ground to work. Truly, there is a great deal to be done in analyzing, working with, and adding to this new framework, the rewards of which cannot yet even be determined.

---

* Remember that the only thing gained by diversification, i.e., trading more than one scenario spectrum, or working in more than two dimensions, is that you increase T, the number of holding periods in a given period of time—you do not reduce risk. In light of this, someone looking to maximize the marginal increase in gain to a marginal increase in *risk*, may well opt to trade only one scenario spectrum.

DRAWDOWN MANAGEMENT AND THE NEW FRAMEWORK

Drawdowns occur from one of three means. The first of these, the most common, is a cataclysmic loss on one trade. I started in this business as a margin clerk where my job was to oversee hundreds of accounts. I have worked as a programmer and consultant to many of the largest traders in the world. I have been trading and working around the trading arena for my entire adult life, often with a birds-eye view of the way people operate in and around the markets. I have witnessed many people being obliterated over the course of a single trade. I have plenty of firsthand experience of getting destroyed on a single trade as well.

The common denominator of every single occasion when this has happened has been a lack of liquidity in the market. The importance of liquidity cannot be overemphasized. Liquidity is not something I have been able to quantify. It isn't simply a function of open interest and volume. Further, liquidity need not dry up for long periods of time in order to do tremendous harm. The U.S. Treasury Bond futures were the most liquid contract in the world in 1987. Yet, that, too, was a very arid place for a few days in October of 1987. You must be ever vigilant regarding liquidity.

The second way people experience great drawdowns is the common, yet even more tragic, means of not knowing their position until the market has moved ferociously against them. This is tragic because, in all cases, this can be avoided. Yet it is a common occurrence. You must always know your position in every market.

The third cause of drawdowns is the most feared, although the consequences are the same as with the first two causes. This type of drawdown is characterized by a protracted losing streak, maybe with some occasional winning trades interspersed between many losers. This is the type of drawdown most traders live in eternal fear of. It is this type of drawdown that makes systems traders question whether or not their systems are still working. However, this is exactly the type of drawdown that can be managed and greatly buffered through the new framework.

The new framework in asset allocation concerns itself with growth optimality. However, the money management community, as a general rule, holds growth optimality as a secondary concern. The primary concern for the money management community is *capital preservation.*

This is true not only of money managers, but of most investors as well. Capital preservation is predicated upon reducing drawdowns. The new framework presented allows us for the first time to reduce the activity of drawdown minimization to a mathematical exercise. This is one of the many fortuitous consequences of—and the great irony of—the new framework.

Everything I have written of in the past and in this book pertains to growth optimality. Yet, in constructing a framework for viewing things in a growth optimal sense, we are able to view things in a drawdown optimal sense within the same framework. The conclusions derived therefrom are conclusions which otherwise would not have been arrived at.

The notion of optimal f, which has evolved into this new framework in asset allocation, can now go beyond the theoretical formulations and concepts and into the real-world implementation to achieve the goals of money managers and individual investors alike.

The older mean-variance models were ill-equipped to handle the notion of drawdown management. The first reason for this is that risk is reduced to the simplified notion that dispersion in returns constitutes risk. It is possible, in fact quite common, to reduce dispersion in returns yet not reduce drawdowns.

Imagine two components that have a correlation to each other that is negative. Component 1 is up on Monday and Wednesday, but down on Tuesday and Thursday. Component 2 is exactly the opposite, being down on Monday and Wednesday, but up on Tuesday and Thursday. On Friday, both components are down. Trading both components together reduces the dispersion in returns, yet on Friday the drawdown experienced can actually be worse than just trading one of the two components alone. *Ultimately, all correlations reduce to one.* The mean variance model does not address drawdowns, and simply minimizing the dispersion in returns, although it may buffer many of the drawdowns, still leaves you open to severe drawdowns.

To view drawdowns under the new framework, however, will give us some very useful information. Consider for a moment that drawdown is minimized by not trading (i.e., at $f = 0$). Thus, if we are considering two simultaneous coin toss games, each paying 2:1, growth is maximized at an f value of .23 for each game, while drawdown is minimized at an f value of 0 for both games.

The first important point to recognize about drawdown optimality (i.e., minimizing drawdowns) is that it can be *approached* in trading. The optimal point, unlike the optimal growth point, cannot be achieved unless we do not trade; however, it can be approached. Thus, to minimize drawdowns, that is, to approach drawdown optimality, requires that we use as small a value for f, for each component, as possible. In other words, to approach drawdown optimality, you must hunker down in the corner of the landscape where all f values are near 0.

In something like the 2:1 coin toss games, depicted in Figure 5.11, the peak does not move around. It is a theoretical ideal, and, in itself, can be used as a superior portfolio model to the conventional models.

However, as was mentioned earlier in this text, in the real world of trading, the markets do not conform so neatly to the theoretical ideal. The problem is that, unlike the 2:1 coin toss games shown, the distribution of returns changes through time as market conditions change. The landscape is polymorphic, moving around as market conditions change. The closer you are to where the peak is, the more dramatic the negative effects will be on you when it moves, simply because the landscape is the steepest in the areas nearest the peak. If we were to draw a landscape map, such as the one in Figure 5.11, but only incorporating data over a

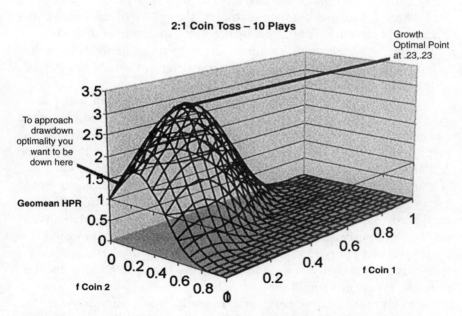

FIGURE 5.11 Drawdown optimality is approached at a different point on the landscape than the growth optimal point.

period when both systems were losing, the landscape (the altitude or TWR) would be at 1.0 at the f coordinates 0,0, and then it would slide off, parabolically, from there.

We approach drawdown optimality by hunkering down in those f values near 0 for all components. In Figure 5.11, we would want to be tucked down in the upper-left corner, near 0 for all f values. The reason for this is that, as the landscape undulates, as the peak moves around, the negative effects on those in that corner are very minimal. In other words, as market conditions *change,* the effect on a trader down in this corner is minimized.

The seeming problem, then, is that growth is sacrificed and this sacrifice in growth occurs with an exponential difference. However, the solution to this problem can be found by the fundamental equation for trading. Since growth—i.e., TWR—is the geometric mean holding period return to the power T, the number of plays is given by:

$$TWR = G^T \qquad\qquad [5.23]$$

By hiding out in the corner, we have a much smaller G. However, by increasing T, i.e., the number of trades, the effect of an exponential decrease in growth is countered, by itself an exponential function.

In short, if a trader must minimize drawdowns, he or she is far better off to trade at a very low f value and get off many more holding periods in the same span of time.

For example, consider playing only one of the 2:1 coin toss games. After 40 holding periods, at the optimal f value of .25, the geometric mean HPR is 1.060660172, and the TWR is 10.55. If we were to play this same game with an f value of .01, our geometric mean HPR would be 1.004888053, which crosses 10.55 when raised to the power of 484. Thus, if you can get off 484 plays (holding periods) in the same time it would take you to get off 40 plays, you would see equivalent growth, with a dramatic reduction in drawdowns. Further, you would have insulated yourself tremendously from changes in the landscape. That is, you would also have insulated yourself a great deal from changing market conditions.

It may appear that you want to trade more than one component (i.e., scenario spectrum) simultaneously. That is, to increase T, you want to trade many more components simultaneously. This is counter to the idea presented on page 192 in discussing the points of inflection that you may be better off to trade only one component. However, by increasing the number of components traded simultaneously, you increase the composite f of the portfolio. For example, if you were to trade 20 scenario spectrums simultaneously, each with a .005 value of f, you would have a composite f of the entire portfolio of 0.1. At such a level, if the worst-case scenarios were to manifest simultaneously, you would experience a 10% drawdown on equity. By contrast, you are better off to trade only one scenario spectrum whereby you can get off the equivalent of 20 holding periods in the same span of time. This may not be possible, but it is the direction you want to be working in to minimize drawdowns.

Finally, when a trader seeks to approach drawdown minimization, he or she can use the continuous dominance notion in doing so. Continuous dominance is great in the theoretical ideal model. However, it is extremely sensitive to changes in the landscape. That is, as the scenarios used as input change to accommodate changing market characteristics, continuous dominance begins to run into trouble. In a gambling game where the conditions do not change from one period to the next, continuous dominance is ideal. In the real world of trading, you must insulate yourself from the undulations in the landscape. Thus, drawdown minimization under the new framework lends itself very well to implementing continuous dominance.

So we have now gone full circle, from discerning the landscape of leverage space and finding the growth optimal point on it to retreating away from that point to approach the real-world primary constraint of drawdown minimization and capital preservation. By simply increasing the exponent, by whatever means available to us, we achieve growth. We can possibly achieve equivalent growth if we can get a high enough T, a high enough exponent. Since the exponent is the number of holding periods in a given span of time, we want to get as many holding periods in a given span of time as possible. This does not necessarily mean, however, to trade as many components as possible. All correlations revert to one. Further, we must always assume that worst-case scenarios will manifest simultaneously for all components traded. We must consider that the composite f, the sum of the f values for all components being simultaneously traded, is a drawdown that we will, therefore, experience. This suggests that, in seeking to approach drawdown optimality, yet still striving for equivalent growth as at the growth optimal point, we trade as few components as possible, with as small an f for each component as possible, while managing to get as many holding periods in a given span of time as possible.

The growth optimal point is a dangerous place to be. However, if we hit it just right, that is, if we are at the place where the peak will be, we can see tremendous growth. Even so, we will endure severe drawdowns. However, the leverage space framework allows us to formulate a plan, a place to be on the map of leverage space, to achieve drawdown minimization. It further allows us an alternate avenue to achieve growth, by increasing T, the exponent, by whatever means necessary. This strategy is not so mathematically obvious when viewed under the earlier frameworks.

A NEW ROLE FOR THE INVESTMENT ANALYST

Ultimately, the investment decision rests entirely with the accuracy of the probabilities assigned to the scenarios. Since we are looking at what percentage to invest in an opportunity, we are not looking at things in the simple Boolean sense. That is, we are not looking at things in the sense of "Should I invest in this or not?" Remember our two-to-one coin toss example from the first part of this book. Conventional wisdom has it that we should invest in this opportunity—that we should take the bet, because it has a positive (arithmetic) mathematical expectation. However, we do not benefit by investing in this opportunity beyond 25%. At 50% and beyond, we will, with certainty, go broke. We should not look at opportunities in the simple Boolean sense of whether or not to invest, whether or not to buy this stock. Rather, we must look at things in the gray-area sense of "How much do I invest in this opportunity?" (and this *can* be 0% or 100%, or most likely in between these two Boolean extremes). Thus, when we consider investing in the stock market, the question is not one of "Should we?" rather it is one of "*How much should we?*"

This new framework presented in this text requires that you think in a non-Boolean sense. The Boolean sense is one in which you are either invested in something (i.e., a value of one), or you are not (i.e., a value of zero). This new framework requires that you think in a non-Boolean sense; that is, the question is no longer "Are you invested (long) in this market?" Rather, it becomes "What percentage are you invested (long) in this market?", where 0% and 100% are possible answers, but more frequently, the exact mathematical answer (considering the possible scenarios for this market) will be a precise value in between zero and one.

Now we know, for a given scenario set or multiple scenario sets, we can mathematically determine the optimal amount to invest. That has been set forth in this book. It is exact, provided the inputs—the scenarios, their outcomes, and probabilities of occurrence—are correct. The results are only as correct as the inputs. Since, in assigning possible scenarios to the way an opportunity may work out, all scenarios are possible, the only guesswork that need be done is in the probabilities we assign. Thus, *ultimately, the investment decision rests entirely with the accuracy of the probabilities assigned.* This is not so easily done, in that we cannot verify the assigned probabilities after the fact. That is, at the end of a holding period, one of the scenarios has been realized. Yet, you cannot know if the probability you assigned to it before its realization is correct or not, much along the lines of Steinbeck's quote at the opening of this book. Market analysis, therefore, should not have as its main goal the question of whether to invest or not. Rather, market analysis should have as its main goal the answers to the far more important questions of "What are the probabilities of this market doing a certain thing?" Solving questions of this sort will yield far more to the investor or money manager in the long run than any market prognostications.

So, it seems we've gone full circle here, from stating that market analysis, technical or otherwise, is no more important than the decision of what quantity to invest. However, it appears that this decision regarding quantity can be answered by our market analysis, *provided* we use the market analysis to assign accurate probabilities to possibilities of what given markets *might* do, as opposed to what we think they *will* do.

REFERENCE

1. Gary P. Brinson, Brian D. Singer, and Gilbert L. Beebower, "Determinants of Portfolio Performance II: An Update," *Financial Analysts Journal* **47,** May–June 1991, pp. 40–49.

Bibliography and Sources

Bellman, Richard, *Adaptive Control Processes,* Princeton: Princeton University Press, 1961.

Brinson, Gary P.; Singer, Brian D.; and Beebower, Gilbert L., "Determinants of Portfolio Performance II: an update," *Financial Analysts Journal* 47, May–June, 1991 pp. 40–49.

Feller, William, *An Introduction to Probability Theory and Its Application,* Vol. II, New York: John Wiley & Sons, 1966.

Gehm, Fred, *Commodity Market Money Management.* New York: Ronald Press, John Wiley & Sons, 1983.

Kelly, J. L., Jr.; "A New Interpretation of Information Rate," *Bell System Technical Journal,* July, 1956, pp. 917–926.

Kuhn, Thomas S.; *The Structure of Scientific Revolutions,* The University of Chicago Press, 1962.

Press, William H.; Flannery, Brian P.; Teukolsky, Saul A.; and Vetterling, William T., *Numerical Recipes: The Art of Scientific Computing,* New York: Cambridge University Press, 1986.

Raiffa, Howard, and Schlaifer, Robert, *Applied Statistical Decision Theory,* Boston: Harvard University, 1961.

Samuelson, Paul A., "The 'Fallacy' of Maximizing the Geometric Mean in Long Sequences of Investing or Gambling," *Proc. Nat. Acad. Sci. USA,* Vol. 68, No. 10, October, 1971, pp. 2493–2496.

Shannon, C. E., "A Mathematical Theory of Communication," *Bell System Technical Journal,* October, 1948, pp. 379–423, 623–656.

Tewles, Richard J.; Harlow, Charles V.; and Stone, Herbert L., *The Commodity Futures Game, Who Wins? Who Losses? Why?,* New York: McGraw-Hill Book Company, 1977.

Thorp, Edward O, *Beat the Dealer,* New York: Vintage Books, Random House, Inc., 1966.

Thorp, Edward O, "The Kelly Money Management System," *Gambling Times,* Dec. 1980, pp. 91–92.

Thorp, Edward O, "The Mathematics of Gambling." *Gambling Times,* Hollywood, California, 1984.

Vince, Ralph, *The Mathematics of Money Management,* New York: John Wiley & Sons, 1992.

Vince, Ralph, *Portfolio Management Formulas,* New York: John Wiley & Sons, 1990.

von Neumann, John, and Morgenstern, Osker, *Theory of Games and Economic Behavior,* Princeton: Princeton University Press, 1944.

Wentworth, R. C., "A Theory of Risk Management Under Favorable Uncertainty," unpublished. 8072 Broadway Terrace, Oakland, CA 94611.

Wentworth, R. C., "Utility, Survival, and Time: Decision Strategies Under favorable Uncertainty," unpublished. 8072 Broadway Terrace, Oakland, CA 94611.

INDEX